Carol Harris is an independent consultant and trainer. Her practice, Management Magic, runs NLP-based courses in many areas of personal and business development, including personal effectiveness, presentation skills, facilitation skills, sales, negotiating and customer care.

Carol is a Sociology graduate, and a Fellow of the Institute of Personnel and Development and of the Institute of Management Consultants. She is a Master Practitioner of NLP, Chair of the UK Association for Neuro-Linguistic Programming and Editor of its quarterly magazine, *Rapport*.

She is author of the 'Success in Mind' series of audiotapes on personal effectiveness, which include the titles: *Super Self, Handling Social Situations, Active Job Seeking, Creating a Good Impression* and *Super Slimming*. She has also written numerous articles for magazines and journals in the UK.

The *Elements of* is a series designed to present high quality introductions to a broad range of essential subjects.

The books are commissioned specifically from experts in their fields. They provide readable and often unique views of the various topics covered, and are therefore of interest both to those who have some knowledge of the subject, as well as to those who are approaching it for the first time.

Many of these concise yet comprehensive books have practical suggestions and exercises which allow personal experience as well as theoretical understanding, and offer a valuable source of information on many important themes.

In the same series

The Aborigine Tradition
Aikido
Alchemy
The Arthurian Tradition
Astrology
The Bahá'í Faith
Buddhism
Celtic Christianity
The Celtic Tradition
The Chakras
Christian Symbolism
Creation Myth
Dreamwork
The Druid Tradition
Earth Mysteries
Egyptian Wisdom
Feng Shui
Gnosticism
The Goddess
The Grail Tradition
Graphology
Handreading
Herbalism
Hinduism
Human Potential

The I Ching
Islam
Judaism
Meditation
Mysticism
Native American Traditions
Natural Magic
NLP
Numerology
Pendulum Dowsing
Prophecy
Psychosynthesis
The Qabalah
Reincarnation
The Runes
Shamanism
Sufism
Tai Chi
Taoism
The Tarot
Unitarianism
Visualization
World Religions
Yoga
Zen

> **the elements of**

nlp
carol harris

Shaftesbury, Dorset • Boston, Massachusetts • Melbourne, Victoria

© Element Books Limited 1998
Text © Carol Harris 1998

First published in Great Britain in 1998 by
Element Books Limited
Shaftesbury, Dorset SP7 8BP

Published in the USA in 1998 by
Element Books, Inc.
160 North Washington Street, Boston, MA 02114

Published in Australia in 1998 by
Element Books
and distributed by Penguin Australia Ltd
487 Maroondah Highway, Ringwood, Victoria 3134

Reprinted 1999

Cover design by Max Fairbrother
Design by Roger Lightfoot
Typeset by WestKey Limited, Falmouth, Cornwall
Printed and bound in Great Britain by
Biddles Limited, Guildford and King's Lynn

British Library Cataloguing in Publication
Data available

Library of Congress Cataloging in Publication
Data available

ISBN 1–86204–323–X

CONTENTS

ACKNOWLEDGEMENTS

This book is dedicated to David Gordon, whose humour, imagination and structured thinking makes NLP both logical and fun.

I would also like to thank the following people, whose assistance in producing this book has been invaluable: Paul Harris, for much of the research and support, Martin Roberts, for being a mine of information on NLP's chequered history, and Katrina Patterson, for her ongoing encouragement and assistance.

My thanks also go to my two NLP 'role models': Roy Johnson, who ran the very first NLP course I ever attended, and Douglas Pride, whose unique blend of humour, concern and entertainment is a real inspiration.

PREFACE

My first encounter with NLP was reading the book which many others had acquired as their primer – *Frogs into Princes*. This book was both fascinating and confusing and, by leaving so many questions unanswered, it became the impetus to further study and the focus of my professional life centring on NLP.

If this book adds to the store of available knowledge on the subject of NLP, I hope it does so utilizing two concepts which have been important to me personally: structure and simplicity. I have aimed to make the book as straightforward as possible; I have also aimed to use a structure which is easy to follow and where specific items can be pursued without having to wade through irrelevancies and jargon.

I would also suggest another key in reading this book; that is curiosity. Curiosity has long been a cornerstone of NLP. Attitudes of curiosity and exploration have led to the major developments which established NLP as a field in its own right and it is these same attitudes which continue to inform its progress.

FINDING YOUR WAY AROUND THIS BOOK

Welcome to *The Elements of NLP*. This book is designed to give you an introduction to the development, techniques and applications of the subject. There are two main sections: Section 1 is about the origins and development of NLP and contains information on its history, notable people and relevant frameworks, models and techniques. Section 2 is about applications and how you can use NLP in your own life. This section includes three broad areas: personal growth, social relationships and business situations.

The appendices outline practical steps you can take if you wish to find out more about NLP, make use of the services of NLP-trained practitioners or pursue professional training in NLP yourself.

Each section has a brief introduction outlining what is included and giving an overview of the topics covered. A more detailed explanation then follows.

The book can be read in a variety of ways, as each part has been designed to stand alone as well as to integrate with the rest of the book. You can choose to read it from start to finish, or you can select those sections which interest you most. If you prefer, you can look at the applications chapters first and then go back to read about the origins. A few topics are mentioned in more than one part of the book; this is intended to make the various sections as self-contained as possible.

NLP is very grounded in experience and it is recommended that you take time to do some of the exercises and activities covered in the applications chapters. This will make the subject more real for you and give you a feel for how NLP actually works in practice; with some of the exercises you may find it helpful to work through them with another person. You might also like to create a personal action plan, which will help you bring what you learn into everyday use.

I hope you enjoy finding out about this fascinating subject, which has made a tremendous impact on so many people's lives.

SECTION ONE

This part of the book is about the history and development of NLP. Chapter 1 begins with some definitions of NLP and then goes on to put NLP in the broader context of developmental approaches. Chapter 2 covers the history of NLP and the contribution made by some of the notable figures in the NLP world. Chapter 3 introduces some of the best-known NLP frameworks, models and techniques.

1 • WHAT IS NEURO-LINGUISTIC PROGRAMMING?

This chapter introduces you to Neuro-Linguistic Programming (NLP) and gives an outline of its scope, its approaches and its features. It also considers its links with other disciplines and some common misconceptions about it.

You probably already 'do' NLP. This is because NLP has its roots in real life behaviour rather than in theory and research. NLP is about how people become successful at things; how they enhance their lives so they can achieve what they aim for. NLP encompasses a wide variety of processes and techniques, and has an overriding emphasis and approach – that of curiosity, exploration and action. NLP can offer you many things, but it helps if you are willing to be adventurous, open to change and fascinated by life and all that it brings.

NLP's main aim is to help people get better at what they do. Its focus on performance has a number of principles, some of which are as follows:

- Excellence in performance can be modelled (analysed) and transferred from one person to another.

- High performance requires both the development of skills and the development of corresponding mental and physical states.
- Mental and physical states can be broken down into small, distinct, elements and modified to achieve desired results.

What distinguishes NLP from many other disciplines is its focus on modelling (*see* chapter 3). Briefly, modelling is the elicitation of sets of patterns; in NLP, patterns which demonstrate how people achieve excellence in performance and which can be copied by others in order to replicate the achievements of high performers. Characteristic features of NLP are its specific techniques for analysing the components of performance, especially how the mind processes information, and its methods of installing strategies for achievement. It can do this across all areas of personal and professional performance, including motivation, learning, maintaining good health, sports performance, communications, negotiating, public speaking, teambuilding and change management.

It should be noted that NLP's processes of modelling are distinct from NLP's applications (for example techniques for enhancing sales, negotiating, teaching and so forth). Many people believe that NLP *is* its techniques, but the techniques are simply a minor part of a field of study which is, in essence, a holistic and systemic approach to understanding personal and organizational effectiveness.

Richard Bandler, co-founder of NLP, has been quoted as saying that, to master NLP, it is necessary to 'let it completely permeate your thinking and feeling' and that it involves 'a ferocious spirit of "going for it" – characteristics of "excitement", "curiosity", "high level state management of moods", "passion" and "commitment" ', (Michael L Hall, *The Spirit of NLP*, The Anglo-American Book Co Ltd, 1996). John Grinder, co-founder of NLP, says that people wanting to train or represent NLP in any way 'need to possess qualities of personal congruity, sparkling intelligence, a deep bottomless curiosity, a driving desire to discover new patterning, a phobic class response to repeating themselves, a continuous scanning for evidence that they are mistaken in every aspect

4

of their personal and professional beliefs, solid personal ethics, physical fitness, actual real world experience in any field in which they intend to present NLP and an excellent sense of humour'. (Internet interview – Inspirative 1996).

NLP provides ways of helping anyone become more competent at what they do, more in control of their thoughts, feelings and actions, more positive in their approach to life and better able to achieve results. If people do not have, within themselves, the knowledge or resources to achieve what they want, NLP makes it possible for them to adapt other people's skills and ways of thinking and incorporate them within their own lives in order to be more successful. NLP is, as one definition has succinctly put it, 'The Art and Science of Excellence'.

DEFINITIONS

Because of its nature, different people perceive different things in NLP and gain different things from it; the definitions, therefore, are numerous and varied. As well as the one given above, definitions have included the following:

- an attitude which is an insatiable curiosity about human beings with a methodology that leaves behind it a trail of techniques (Richard Bandler)
- an owner's guide to the mind
- the study of subjective experience
- the study of the structure of subjectivity
- software for the brain
- a new Science of Achievement
- the study of human excellence
- the ability to be your best more often
- a manual for the structured use of creativity
- an adventure in experience

Most of these definitions focus on personal improvement and, whereas other disciplines, such as psychology, give insights into human behaviour and motivation, NLP actually provides practical ways of improving performance. So it incorporates a technology for bringing about change in people; a set of approaches and tools which combine to offer ideas and skills for enhancing how people do things.

Putting this simply, NLP helps people identify their present states (how they think and feel, what they do and the results they achieve), consider their desired states (what they would really like instead), then move from one to the other. It is not prescriptive about what the desired states should be, leaving that to the individual. For example, two people might both wish to become better at responding to other people's criticism. They might both become upset (their 'present state') when criticized, but the first person might wish to 'be able to accept criticism in a positive way', while the second person might wish to 'be able to use the criticism to bring about personal change'. These are different 'desired states' and both people could be helped to achieve their aims, but NLP does not tell them that one aim is 'correct' or 'more desirable' than another (although it can help them consider the advantages and disadvantages of each).

To achieve the transition from present state to desired state, there are three elements which NLP considers: *you* (your own situation and disposition); *others* (those with whom you are dealing) and *flexibility* (the possibility of varying what you do in order to be effective).

ORIGINS

We will be covering the history of NLP in the next chapter; the following is just a very brief outline to put the rest of this chapter into context.

NLP originated in the early 1970s in the USA, although much of it was based on approaches which were considerably older. The contribution of the founders of NLP as a discrete field of study was twofold: first, the codification, enlargement and extension of previously existing concepts into a practically useful developmental tool and, secondly, the promotion of 'modelling' (*see* chapter 3) to replicate excellence in performance.

NLP stands for Neuro-Linguistic Programming, a title given to it by its major founders, Richard Bandler and John Grinder, although the term 'neuro-linguistic' had been coined by Korzybski much earlier and appeared in print in his book *Science and Sanity* in 1933. *Neuro* relates to the mind and how it works; *linguistic* relates to the ways in which people express their experience of the world; *programming* relates to the fact that people behave according to personal 'programmes' which govern their ways of being in the world. So NLP encompasses the ways in which people think and act in their everyday lives.

California in the 1970s was a hotbed of ideas and activities. Richard Bandler and John Grinder (*see* chapter 2) began exploring how really effective people achieved their results. They turned their attention to a number of individuals, each of whom excelled in their own field and three of whom, in particular, were the subjects of most publicity – Milton Erickson, Virginia Satir and Fritz Perls (*see* chapter 2).

In studying these people who excelled in their professions, Bandler and Grinder were curious to explore what was the 'difference that made the difference' – in other words what, specifically, led these people to excel. They found that each of their subjects exhibited specific personal patterns of behaviour and thinking, and it is these patterns, with their component elements, which form much of the basis for NLP.

So what are the elements involved in people's patterns? Although not originally put into a specific unified model, certain discrete elements are involved; in particular thoughts, feelings and behaviour. In other words how people THINK, how they FEEL and what they DO; these three elements are the foundation of performance. Other elements can be added, in particular *objectives*, *beliefs/values/assumptions* and *spirituality*. In taking these elements as key, I have drawn upon the work of David Gordon, Graham Dawes and Robert Dilts and the next part of this chapter is based especially on the Experiential Dynamics model of Gordon and Dawes – *see* chapter 3.

What Bandler, Grinder and their colleagues noticed was that the people they studied had ways of thinking, feeling

7

and behaving which made them effective. The people were not always personally aware of these patterns, but they could be noticed by keen outside observers. The conclusions reached were that once you can observe and describe such patterns, they can be copied by others. This meant that other people could learn to follow the same patterns in order to achieve similar results.

Now there is nothing startlingly new in this process; it is how much learning takes place. For example, for a child to learn how to tie a shoelace, it has to copy (model) how someone else does it. What makes NLP particularly effective is its ability to break down performance into very small elements and take account of 'internal' processes, such as thoughts and feelings, as well as 'external' behaviour, when helping others to learn and develop.

UTILIZING AND WORKING WITH THE PATTERNS

If we take each element in turn, we can see how NLP enables people to explore and enhance their performance. Later we will be returning to some of these approaches and showing how you can use them personally in your own development.

OBJECTIVES

There are already well-established approaches to objective setting; for example the SMART approach (*see* chapter 6). NLP goes beyond these, and helps define objectives in a way which makes it much more likely that they will be achieved. To do this, NLP uses what it calls Well Formed Outcomes (WFO), which is a model for setting effective objectives. This model is covered in detail in chapter 6 and is the foundation for effective NLP work; by ensuring that objectives are well defined, progress and change are facilitated.

BEHAVIOUR

Behaviour is the only thing which is observable by others; they cannot see into your mind or know how you are feeling unless you either tell them or show them – and both of these are behaviour. So NLP works with all aspects of behaviour, helping people to observe and respond to behaviour in useful and appropriate ways.

Some specific ways in which NLP works with behaviour are the following:

- **Helping people to learn skills**. This often involves 'role modelling' someone with excellent skills in a particular field and learning how to transfer these skills to another person. Examples of this could include playing a musical instrument (finding out which techniques are used by professional musicians and emulating them) or taking part in sports (selecting top performers in different sporting fields – eg golf, athletics, tennis – and breaking down their performance into component parts in order to replicate it).
- **Creating and maintaining rapport and influence**. NLP has specific ways of enhancing rapport and influence; notably the concept of 'matching' (or copying) other people in order to make them feel at ease. The idea is that most people feel comfortable with others who are similar to themselves, so by making yourself a little more like other people you can enhance their feelings of comfort and acceptance (*see also* chapter 5).
- **Using language to communicate and influence**. There are a number of aspects here, including the following:

  - recognizing people's personality and motivational patterns through their language patterns
  - recognizing which senses people rely on, through listening to the actual words they use
  - being able to use either precise or general language where appropriate to achieve particular results
  - using indirect language for persuasiveness and influence
  - respecting the actual words and phrases used by individuals, as those words represent their experience of reality

We will return to language in Chapters 4–6.

THINKING

The elements of thought involve seeing (visualizing), hearing (imagining sounds or having 'internal conversations' or dialogue in one's head), experiencing sensations (emotional or tactile) and sensing smells or tastes. In each of these areas, NLP enables people to notice their thoughts and then, if needed, to modify them.

For example, you might ask someone to think about a flower. First he can imagine how the flower looks (its colour and shape), then imagine how it smells (its scent), then imagine how it feels (its form and texture), then imagine how it sounds (perhaps its leaves rustling in a breeze), then imagine how it tastes (some flowers are edible!). So far, the experience has been imitating reality – you have asked the person to imagine a real flower, as it is usually perceived. Now for the interesting part; you can ask the person to manipulate his mental experience to create something entirely new. So, for example, you might ask him to imagine the flower a different colour, a different size, with a different smell, making an unusual sound, and so forth. The ability of the mind to make these changes is a foundation for learning and innovation and, if you have never experimented in such a manner, you may be amazed at the changes in experience which such mental shifts can bring about.

Because of its ability to manipulate the senses, NLP can help people create more, or less, pleasant experiences for themselves. And in case you are wondering why they should want to create a less pleasant experience, think of how to teach people to avoid putting their hands into fire, or how to make sure they do not drive after they have been drinking.

FEELINGS

NLP was largely founded on the activities of therapists and it has continued to emphasize the importance of a balanced emotional state in achieving effective performance. It has techniques for managing emotions, many of them involving the sensory shifts referred to in the previous section.

Emotional responses are often brought about by thoughts and are certainly closely linked to them, so by changing thought patterns it is often possible to change emotional responses.

Another way in which NLP engages the emotions is through its association with behaviour. Because there is a close link between body and mind, by making changes in the body, changes in the mind – and thereby the emotions – often follow. An example of this is posture. Most people have habitual postures associated with different emotional states, for example being more upright when energetic and taking up less space when apprehensive. By changing posture it is possible to change the thoughts and feelings which follow. So to get someone to feel more energetic, it is possible to identify their personal posture for energy and then help them re-create it; once they have done so, they are more likely to feel energetic. The same goes for states such as calmness, relaxation, motivation, enthusiasm and so forth – certain postures are more likely to produce each of these states in a given person.

BELIEFS/VALUES/ASSUMPTIONS

One of NLP's strengths is its ability to influence change at deep levels. Although change can be brought about by teaching people new skills, it is beliefs, values and assumptions which are the foundation of each individual.

Much of NLP is about changes in beliefs, values and assumptions, sometimes direct and sometimes indirect. For example, a direct belief change could be brought about by confronting a person with an example which contradicts her previous experience; maybe showing her a yellow tomato if she believed tomatoes were always red or encouraging a person from a minority group to apply for (and get) a senior job which she had believed was beyond his reach. An indirect belief change could be brought about through exposing a person to different learning situations which, cumulatively, resulted in her changing her beliefs; for example giving a person who believed she was poor at public speaking the opportunity to practise until she was convinced she could do it. Equally, assumptions may be changed when a person gains

11

a different perspective on a situation; for example a person who thinks a neighbour is being indifferent to her, but then finds out the person is slightly deaf and has not been able to hear what she is saying.

The interesting thing about the way in which NLP works to effect such changes is that it can help people experience changes in their mind, rather than having to put them in 'real life' situations to face real (or imagined) obstacles. It has even been claimed that people have actual mental 'locations' for beliefs and that by helping people to locate and utilize these locations, it is possible to influence the strength of their beliefs.

SPIRITUALITY

NLP also offers ways of exploring what is 'beyond' everyday experience. Spirituality is a rather different concept from the other elements we have been discussing, ie behaviour, thoughts, feelings and beliefs. These elements are easier to communicate, as people are likely to have more of a shared understanding of them. For example, in discussing behaviour, it is relatively easy to assess whether a shop assistant has been helpful or uninterested, or whether a student is listening or distracted; these things are relatively easy to observe and construe. With spirituality, however, each person's experience is both 'internal' and personal and the vocabulary with which to discuss it is frequently more limited.

For example, two people may visit an area of countryside where they can enjoy seeing the landscape, hearing the sounds of animals, feeling the sunshine and being aware of the scents in the air. One person may simply experience this as a pleasant day out; for the other person, the outing may give him an awareness of something beyond the immediate experience; perhaps a sense of fulfilment, of integration, or of a power or quality which permeates his senses. While being acutely conscious of this personal experience, it may be difficult for the second person to explain in everyday language what his awareness actually is.

Despite such limitations, many people working with NLP are helping others to develop their spiritual sense and awareness.

FEATURES OF NLP

NLP has some specific features which mark it out; other disciplines may have one or more of these, but the combination of all makes NLP distinctive. What are these features?

IT TAKES A HOLISTIC APPROACH

NLP takes the view that all parts of a person are interrelated and that changes in one part reflect on all the others. This approach ensures that the overall consequences of any change process are considered.

IT WORKS WITH MICRO-DETAILS

In contrast to being holistic, NLP is also often concerned with minute detail. An example of this is the way in which it works with specific elements of thought processes, such as how people visualize and how they use 'internal dialogue'. NLP enables people to analyse such processes in a way that helps them be more effective. Working with detail often helps understanding and assimilation and makes it possible to work on one element at a time, rather than being swamped by multiple activities all together.

IT IS COMPETENCY- AND ROLE-MODELLING-BASED

NLP is very much to do with individual skills and abilities. In this respect it ties in well with current approaches to training and development. The foundation of NLP is 'modelling' (*see* chapter 3), especially 'role modelling' effective people; finding out precisely which elements of their performance are contributing to their success, and then training others to perform in a similar manner.

The Elements of NLP

Although a good deal of NLP is about behaviour, much of it is about how people's thoughts influence their performance. NLP offers ways of modifying mental patterns (or strategies) and helping people make changes in these to help enhance their lives.

IT UTILIZES SPECIFIC LANGUAGE PATTERNS

Utilization of language patterns provides powerful techniques for interacting with others and bringing about change.

IT WORKS WITH BOTH THE CONSCIOUS AND THE UNCONSCIOUS MIND

The terms 'conscious' and 'unconscious' have been used in various parts of this book. The state of consciousness is generally recognizable as an awareness of oneself or elements in one's environment (or beyond).

The term 'unconscious' is commonly applied to states such as sleep, anaesthesia or fainting, but can also be used to describe mental processes which are 'out of awareness'. These 'out of awareness' processes can include a wide range of things; for example having a mannerism of which one is not consciously aware, becoming familiar with a language simply by being exposed to hearing it rather than consciously taking time to learn the words or grammar, or responding to something in an automatic way without being aware of why that is happening (for example considering a person attractive because the pupils of the eyes are dilated, but not being aware of that fact as influencing your reaction).

Although there are differing views on how, or whether, unconscious processes actually exist (they could simply be preprogrammed behaviour rather than evidence of an 'unconscious' part of the mind), there is a general acceptance that the unconscious mind does exist and has a powerful influence on our attitudes and behaviour. This influence may be either positive or negative, resulting in behaviour which either achieves beneficial results or hinders them. The recognition of the influence of the unconscious mind informs much of NLP's work so that, although it is possible to use NLP to work solely at a conscious level, for example to break down a skill into concrete parts in order to teach it, it is probably most effective when it integrates conscious/unconscious processing. For example, when teaching a skill to people who believe that they will find it hard to learn, it is possible to manage the process of teaching so that it incorporates elements which reach the unconscious mind and are directly absorbed by the learner at a deep level.

A note of caution should be added here. Because some techniques appear to work directly at an unconscious level, bypassing conscious awareness, they could be open to misuse or could inadvertently cause undesirable results. Such techniques should therefore only be used after sufficient training and with the safeguards of respect and concern for the person who is 'on the receiving end'. For this reason, certain techniques have only been described in outline in this book, so that they will not be practised without sufficient guidance and skill.

IT IS RAPID IN ITS PROCESSES AND RESULTS

A major feature of NLP is the speed with which it can produce results. Many NLP techniques are extremely rapid in their application (the most famous probably being the 'fast phobia cure', which can successfully be carried out in a matter of minutes; because of its speed, many people do not believe it can really work and are therefore sceptical about NLP as a whole. Current thinking, however, is that the brain works (and learns) speedily and therefore change can be brought about rapidly. This is in contradiction to many traditional approaches, especially psychotherapy, which maintain that lengthy courses of treatment – often running into years – are necessary to bring about insight and change.

IT IS NEUTRAL AS AN APPROACH

NLP as an approach is neutral. It is a tool, not a prescription. How it is used depends entirely on the practitioner and the user/client. There are as many ways of using NLP as there are people working with it.

An interesting thing about NLP is that one of its principles involves respect for others; this is instilled as important from the early stages of training. Because of this, attention is paid to what is termed 'ecology' which, in NLP, means the circumstances surrounding any particular intervention. To be ecological means paying attention to the needs and wishes of the person with whom you are working and to take into account the other person's point of view and situation as well as your own beliefs about what is desirable. This intrinsic emphasis on ethics makes NLP stand out from many other disciplines.

PRESUPPOSITIONS

Another feature of NLP is its presuppositions. These are statements which are not necessarily held to be 'true', but used as assumptions which influence strongly the behaviour and responses of those using NLP. Here are some of NLP's commonest presuppositions:

- **Experience has structure**. There are patterns to how we think about/organize our experience and, if we change these patterns, our experience changes with it.
- **A map is not the territory**. People's perceptions are subjective, what you perceive is selective and not a complete, or necessarily true, account of reality. So, for example, a colour blind person would not perceive certain distinctions in colour, but this does not mean they do not exist. Similarly, a person might construe another's behaviour as malevolent, but this might not be the case. We see and respond according to our own selectively filtered 'maps of the world' and helping people understand theirs, and acknowledge those of others, is a feature of NLP.
- **The mind and body are one system**. What we do with our minds and our bodies is interlinked. For example, sitting

in a particular posture can lead us to feel a particular emotion; similarly a positive thought will have an effect on our physiology. In current times there has been much emphasis on the interrelations of mind and body on health (for example the use of visualization in helping fight cancer) and psychoneuroimmunology is demonstrating such links on an ongoing basis.

- **People work perfectly**. Instead of thinking of people as faulty because they do not do what seems to be appropriate, conventional or effective, it is useful to think of them as being extremely effective at getting particular results, even though these results may not be the 'best' in the circumstances. So, for example, someone who has a phobia, say of spiders, is excellent at maintaining a frightened response; this may be a real help in keeping away from poisonous spiders in a tropical country, but be inappropriate as a reaction to house spiders.

- **If something is possible for one person it is possible for everybody**. This does not mean that everyone can be an Olympic athlete, brain surgeon or artist; it simply means that if something *can* be done by one person then, *potentially*, everyone could do it, given suitable resources. This pre-supposition is helpful in working with people to encourage them to extend their performance beyond what they might previously have believed possible.

- **Everyone has all the resources they need**. People have within themselves a vast reservoir of abilities and attributes; achievement is generally more about what you bring to a situation than about external elements.

- **There is no failure, only feedback**. If you do not achieve what you set out to, this can be taken as useful information to help in your future endeavours, rather than as evidence that you are incapable of achieving what you desire.

- **If what you are doing is not working, do something else**. Flexibility is a key to effectiveness; if you vary what you do until you get a result, you are more likely to be effective than if you continue to carry out behaviour which is not getting you where you want to be.

- **You do the best you can at the time**. Although, with hindsight, many things could be done differently, we can only make the best choice at the time. This does not mean we always make the 'right' decision; simply that decisions are based on 'best guesses' at the time. ('New code' NLP might take a different view of this and help us listen more to our 'body signals', but more of that in chapter 3.)
- **Every behaviour has a positive intent**. Even the most negative-seeming behaviour is done for a purpose. This is a useful assumption to make when dealing with others, as it enables you to consider why they behave as they do, to explore their real needs and, possibly, to find alternative ways of meeting them.
- **The meaning of the communication is the response it elicits**. It is the perception of the receiver that determines the effectiveness of interaction, not the intention of the initiator.

Almost all the presuppositions have been debated at length, for example the proposal that all behaviour has a positive intent, or the fact that what is possible for one person is potentially possible for all. However, the point of the presuppositions is to enable people to extend themselves and to perceive opportunities and benefits in situations. By acting *as if* the presuppositions were true, it is amazing what can be achieved.

ASSOCIATIONS

Where did NLP come from? Many of the ideas used originated in much earlier times. Certainly many of the concepts were known about decades ago and some were mentioned, although in very different terminology, centuries ago. There are, however, a number of specific connections between NLP and other established disciplines, in particular the following:

- **Applied psychology**. It is easy to think of NLP as a branch of applied psychology. To label it in this way is really to diminish its significance, as it goes beyond the bounds of traditional psychology, but it is probably a good initial way of putting NLP in a wider context. One explanation of how NLP goes beyond conventional psychology has been expressed as follows: 'While traditional clinical psychology is primarily concerned with describing diffi- culties, categorizing them, and searching for historical causes, NLP is interested in *how* our thoughts, actions, and feelings work together right now to produce our expe- rience' (Faulkner). There is also a link with psychometric testing (and some Jungian 'traits') in the use of one of the NLP language patterns called Meta-Programmes (*see* chapter 5).

- **Gestalt Psychology/Psychotherapy**. One of the early role models for NLP was Fritz Perls, the reputed father of Gestalt Psychotherapy. Gestalt relates to the linkages between elements, so that an entity can be understood through the interrelationships of its parts; the parts alone do not neces- sarily make sense. (One area of NLP deals with 'parts' and we will be returning to that concept in chapter 3.)
- **Ericksonian Hypnosis**. Another early role model was Milton Erickson, and his influence on NLP has been enor- mous. Unlike classical hypnosis, the Ericksonian approach is seemingly low-key and unobtrusive. With this approach, much use is made of indirect language, suggestion and utilization of the patient's own patterns of speaking, breathing and moving in order to bring about change. Erickson himself was expert at adapting his approach to the specific needs of the individual with whom he was working and this way of working has informed many of NLP's later practitioners (although Erickson was heavily influenced by classical hypnosis and used many direct techniques himself).
- **Systems thinking/cybernetics**. Much of NLP utilizes systems thinking. Work by Ashby, Beer and others has had a major impact on how NLP has developed and been used and many of the NLP models covered in chapter 3 explore the systemic nature of different areas of experience.
- **Linguistics**. Much of NLP originated in the work of linguists, including Korzybski and Chomsky. Such people had laid down many of the principles which underlie

NLP's language patterns. Some of the connections which have been made are with the ways in which language represents experience, especially in a metaphorical sense, and the ways in which language demonstrates people's underlying motivational and behavioural patterns.

In addition, some topics which are becoming associated with NLP are:

- **Accelerated learning**. Accelerated learning puts much emphasis on the needs of the individual and the helpfulness of recognizing and utilizing individual patterns in order to enhance learning and development. The earliest writer on this topic was the Bulgarian Georgi Lozanov, working in the 1960s. In particular, accelerated learning puts the onus on the trainer to ensure that the learner is in a resourceful state in which to learn, and this means that learning is not simply a one-way process, of pushing information towards a recipient and hoping it will stick, but creating an atmosphere in which interaction and mutual respect can lead to individual growth.
- **Bodywork**. NLP is increasingly being associated with the field of physical development as well as psychological enhancement. Some examples of current links are the Alexander Technique, Feldenkrais, Kinesiology, Tai Chi, Voicework/singing, and so forth. With all these techniques, practitioners use a mix of body movement/activity together with mental/emotional control to achieve results.

NLP constantly draws upon other disciplines and approaches to integrate appropriate parts of them with its own ways of working. Because of this, it is evolving all the time and, while it remains recognizable, is fluid and flexible.

MISCONCEPTIONS

Having explained what NLP is, it is also important to mention what it is not. There are several popular misconceptions about it and the following questions are often asked by people new to NLP:

1 **Is NLP not just positive thinking?** Yes, in a way, but it goes far beyond simply having nice thoughts and actually gives people a way of knowing WHAT to do in order to think positively. For example, some years ago a training video was produced on presentation skills. The video told viewers that it was important, when making a presentation, to *feel confident*. However, no advice was offered on how to do that! NLP makes it possible to offer such advice, by being able to identify specific things which can be done to master thoughts and feelings as well as behaviour.

2 **Is NLP not manipulative?** Many things can be used in a manipulative way, although they themselves are simply neutral tools. For example a motor car can be driven in such a way that it becomes a hazard; a person collecting money for an animal charity could take along a sorry-looking small furry animal, aiming to elicit feelings of sympathy in passers by. NLP as an approach, like the motor car or the small animal, is neutral; it does not impose on its user rules for its use. So how you use NLP is as important as what you use it for; it is ultimately up to you to determine whether it is used ethically or not.

3 **How can NLP be taken seriously if it claims to work so quickly?** The problem with this question is that it presupposes a limited way of thinking. If you are used to things taking a long time, speed may be suspicious. For example, you could say it takes years of study to learn the differences between wild plants, but one encounter with a stinging nettle could well imprint its appearance and smell indelibly on your mind! Because conventional psychological approaches have traditionally been time-consuming, it can be difficult to believe that work with NLP can be as fast as it is; the proof, however, is in the results it achieves.

4 **Is it really a separate field of study?** This question often comes from people used to thinking about subjects in a very tightly defined way and it is sometimes said that NLP draws on so many other disciplines that it is not a discrete field in itself. Although it has drawn upon many other disciplines, NLP does have unique elements of its own, some of which were covered at the beginning of this

21

chapter in the section on 'Features of NLP'. It is probably the focus on the practical applications of mental processing and the importance of modelling which most distinguishes NLP from other disciplines. It also has established programmes of study, with recognized qualifications at different levels, making it a discipline which is unique and identifiable.

THE FUTURE OF NLP

From the beginning, NLP has been evolving and developing. Its main founders are still active and developing new concepts and approaches, as are others newer to the field. For the future, we can anticipate further refinements, more applications and innovation and creativity in NLP's further development.

2 • THE HISTORY OF NLP

In the last chapter, some of the origins of NLP were discussed and some people associated with its development mentioned. This section takes a more in-depth look at these origins, both in the USA and the UK and at some of the people who have been a great influence on the emergence and continuation of NLP; some by contributing new techniques and approaches and some by popularizing NLP to a wider audience.

NLP IN THE USA

NLP as a defined field of study originated in the USA in the early 1970s although, as mentioned in the last chapter, there were many influences on its development, going back decades (including likely links to US Air Force/CIA research on language, modelling, eye movements and so forth) or, in the case of some of the ideas themselves, centuries.

In the late 1950s, a group of people had come together in Palo Alto, California in what became known as the Communication Research Project. Led by Gregory Bateson (*see* below), it studied communications, psychotherapy, brief therapy and animal behaviour. A further group was set up later at the Mental Research Institute (MRI), the best known members of which were Paul Watzlawick and the late David Weakland. This group was generally referred to as the Palo Alto Group. The work at Palo Alto led to further research at Stanford University and was a major influence on the early developers of NLP.

The focus of activity for NLP itself was, initially, the University at Santa Cruz, California, where the Dean had a vision of creating an environment where different disciplines, ideas and models could come together in a creative way. This whole area of California was a hotbed of ideas and development, including Santa Cruz, Palo Alto and Big Sur, where the famous Esalen Institute was formed. In this climate, a group of people became interested in personal enhancement, creativity and communications; the underpinning drive which lay behind most of its activities was that of curiosity.

NLP's main founders, Richard Bandler and John Grinder, were part of the wider group at Santa Cruz, working on aspects of development. Bandler studied various topics – initially physics and computing, later psychology, philosophy and maths. Becoming disillusioned with existing university courses, he explored ways of bringing about practical changes in the fields in which he was working. One of his particular interests was Gestalt Psychology and he started to teach seminars in Gestalt Therapy.

Bandler formed a close association with John Grinder, Assistant Professor of Linguistics. Grinder had gained a PhD in San Francisco, where his language studies included the theories of Noam Chomsky, the American linguist. Grinder had been an interpreter in the US army and been engaged in covert operations. He was very experienced in working with language through modelling (*see* chapter 3), and had learned several languages using this process.

As Bandler had exceptional skills in absorbing other people's behaviour patterns (in the early days he was referred to as a sponge, because of this ability to 'become' another person) and Grinder had great experience of modelling (and was sometimes referred to as a chameleon because of his ability to 'change his colours without changing himself'), they began working together, with Bandler showing Grinder what he did and Grinder helping him model it. Together, they analysed the performance of many people, including some leading therapists – initially Fritz Perls and Virginia Satir, and later Milton Erickson. Although Virginia Satir and Milton Erickson were available face to face, Perls had already died and Bandler's analysis of how he worked came from studying videotapes of him. Together with Bandler and Grinder, a group formed, which met and worked on the various elements which became the foundations of NLP. Each of the emerging techniques was explored and refined on an ongoing basis. As well as working on NLP, people were experimenting with hypnotic techniques and language. Terrence McClendon, in *The Wild Days*, remarks on the association between NLP and hypnosis: 'You could say that the NLP techniques are the conscious mind's model of how the unconscious mind works in hypnosis.'

It is often difficult to attribute the emergence of some particular NLP techniques to a particular 'creator'; the efforts of the whole Santa Cruz group often interrelated in order to allow these forms to emerge. As work continued, the different elements of NLP gradually emerged, and many of its original creators and developers are still making further refinements and extensions.

While they were still working together, Richard Bandler and John Grinder set up the Society of Neuro-Linguistic Programming, originally as a partnership between Bandler's company, Not Limited, and Grinder's, Limited Unlimited. They also formed a publishing company called Meta Publications, which was responsible for many of the notable books in the field of NLP.

In 1977 the Division of Training and Research (DOTAR), a training, development and research operation, was set up in Santa Cruz by Richard Bandler, John Grinder, Judith DeLozier, Leslie Cameron, Maribeth Anderson, Robert Dilts and David Gordon. This was the first NLP training institute and Leslie Cameron was overall Director, David Gordon was Director of Training and Robert Dilts was Director of Research.

As the field grew, so some of the original associations began to change and, in particular, the partnership between Richard Bandler and John Grinder came to an end in the early 1980s. Their interests had begun to diverge and they also had different ideas about what the future held in store for NLP. Both, however, continued to be driving forces within NLP and continue to train and write to this day.

NLP was, from its inception, very much about practicalities and application rather than theory. Questions such as: 'How can this be used?' and 'How can this be taught?' were asked frequently. The legacy of the Santa Cruz group lies, at least in part, in the attitudes of curiosity and usefulness which informed its work. As NLP continues to develop, questions about application and transfer are still foremost in the minds of many working in the field.

NLP IN THE UK

While NLP began life in the USA, the UK took up its development early on and, internationally, is a major focal point for activity, especially in relation to its professionalization. Although other countries are developing their use of NLP, the USA and UK are very much centres for creativity and application, and some of the UK practices (notably the way its professional association is functioning) are being used as models for US developments.

There were two strands to the development of NLP in the UK, beginning in 1979 and involving Eileen Watkins Seymour and Graham Dawes. Together with Gene Early, Ian Cunningham and David Gaster, they made contacts which led to the foundation of the UK Training Centre for Neuro-Linguistic Programming (UKTC). The first Diploma (Practitioner) programme in the UK started, as an eight-month programme, in October 1982; it was the only place offering full-scale NLP training anywhere outside North America. Later, the UKTC was handed over to Dudley and Regan Masters, who had graduated from it some time earlier, but it only lasted for two further years and then wound up.

Following its start, however, other training organizations came into existence until, in the late 1990s, there were around 50 in the UK.

THE ASSOCIATION FOR NEURO-LINGUISTIC PROGRAMMING (ANLP)

Formed in 1985 as a non-profit making organization, ANLP is a professional body which is recognized internationally as probably the leading association for those interested in, and using, NLP. Originally set up by Eileen Whicker following an inaugural meeting at the London Business School on 8 May 1985, it was envisaged as an umbrella organization for the development of NLP, 'setting core standards for training and practice, being a basis for exchanging information and experience, creating links with other NLP bodies, setting standards and ethics, promoting research, keeping abreast of legislation and representing NLP in a professional capacity'.

PEOPLE

Let us now turn to some of the people who were involved in NLP's development, contributed ideas which were seminal to its progress, or helped popularize and promote it as a field of activity.

RICHARD BANDLER AND JOHN GRINDER

As mentioned above, these two men are acknowledged as NLP's 'founding fathers'. Although generally credited with creating NLP, many of the ideas and principles had come from, or been based on the ideas and writings of, earlier thinkers.

ALFRED KORZYBSKI

Recognized as the founding father of general semantics, Count Korzybski had a major effect on the development of NLP and, in particular, the Meta-Model. Born in Warsaw in 1879, he trained as an engineer, served in the First World

War, attached to the General Staff Intelligence Department of the Second Russian Army and later served in the US and Canadian military services. He developed his theory of 'time-binding' around 1921 and published his first book, *Manhood of Humanity* in 1921.

Korzybski was founder and Director of the Institute of General Semantics, established in 1938 as a centre for training in his work, including neuro-linguistic research and education. He was the first person to use the term 'neuro-linguistic', and it appeared in his most famous book, *Science and Sanity* in 1933; he continued to write and lecture until his death in 1950.

NOAM CHOMSKY

Chomsky was a professor of linguistics whose work, based on Korzybski's earlier ideas, was key to much of the development of NLP. Now a revolutionary figure, prominent in US politics, he became very anti-establishment at the time of the Vietnam war. Chomsky's work on general semantics first appeared in a range of published papers and culminated in the 1957 publication – now out of print – *Syntactic Structures*. This work established the transformational model of language, with its concepts of deep structure and surface structure, elements which feature heavily in NLP's approach to precision in language (*see* chapter 3).

GREGORY BATESON

Bateson was a British anthropologist and author who influenced several of NLP's leading proponents. His father, a geneticist who apparently coined the word 'genetics', named Bateson after the Russian geneticist, Gregor Mendel. Bateson, who was married to fellow anthropologist Margaret Mead, was ethnologist at the Veterans Administration Hospital, Palo Alto, and later studied communication in animals in the Virgin Islands and in Hawaii and produced a book, *Steps to an Ecology of Mind*. He wrote on topics including communications, systems theory/cybernetics, psychology, psychiatry, anthropology, biological evolution and genetics and lectured at Santa Cruz when Bandler and Grinder were developing NLP. Bateson said people should think and act systemically, by allowing both conscious and unconscious processes to shape their decisions, and by developing congruity in diverse parts of the mind; this emphasis on systemic thinking has been a vital part of much NLP work. Bateson received a Guggenheim Fellowship for synthesizing cybernetic ideas with anthropological data.

CARLOS CASTANEDA

An anthropologist and writer whose works greatly influenced Bandler and Grinder and their associates, Castaneda's writings made great use of metaphor, often in conversational dialogues, and some of his ideas formed the basis for therapeutic interventions. His thoughts on 'stopping the world' – a concept where the mind is stilled to allow expansion of consciousness, was one of the underpinning elements of New Code NLP (*see* chapter 3.)

ROSS ASHBY, STAFFORD BEER AND PETER CHECKLAND

These systems thinkers and writers have strongly influenced NLP. Ashby originated the law of requisite variety in 1956, emphasizing the importance of continued exploration and creativity regarding variations in the way we work towards results. Beer, an expert on systems, has provided models which can be used with both individuals and organizations and Checkland was the developer of soft systems thinking.

ALBERT ELLIS

A psychotherapist, writer and lecturer and a major influence on people in NLP, especially Dilts and DeLozier. Ellis felt traditional therapy took too long and developed a more active approach (Rational Emotive Therapy – RET). He also used shifts in time in a similar way to NLP (*see* chapter 3.)

ROBERTO ASSAGIOLI

Assagioli is known as the founder of psychosynthesis, on which he published the seminal book in 1965. Recently, his work has been rediscovered and Michael Hall, an American therapist and trainer, wrote on Assagioli's work in the American NLP publication *Anchorpoint*, where he outlined several of Assagioli's ideas and exercises and showed that his work predated NLP by around ten years. Some areas of similarity which Hall points out include what NLP knows as 'Well Formed Outcomes' (objective setting), 'Sub-modalities' (elements of sensory perception), 'Anchoring', 'Swish Techniques', 'Personality Parts' and 'Spiritual Development'. Assagioli is named as one of the possible sources for NLP in Genie Laborde's book *Influencing with Integrity*.

MAXWELL MALTZ

Maltz was a plastic surgeon, writing in the 1960s, again before NLP was 'created'; whose book *Psycho-Cybernetics* contained ideas, references and guidance using numerous techniques which we now regard as NLP.

PAUL WATZLAWICK

Austrian by birth, Watzlawick was a research assistant at the MRI in Palo Alto from 1960, and Clinical Associate Professor at the Department of Psychiatry and Behavioral Sciences at Stanford University Medical Center. He was later Professor of Psychotherapy at the University of El Salvador in Central America. One of his books, *Change*, sets out many of his ideas, which were an invaluable resource to the development of NLP.

VIRGINIA SATIR

As mentioned earlier, Satir was one of the earliest, and best known, people whose ways of working acted as models for the analysis and development of many NLP principles and processes. She was a social worker, particularly interested in family systems, who developed an approach to family therapy called 'conjoint family therapy' and taught the subject at the MRI in Palo Alto, in the first training programme in the country on family therapy.

One of Satir's ways of working was with what she termed 'parts parties', where people would act out characteristics of different facets of personality. A model which is associated with her is her analysis of five different communication patterns (known as 'Satir categories'), which she called 'blamer', 'placator', 'distractor', 'computer' and 'leveller', each having typical postures and modes of communication. These patterns are discussed in her book *Peoplemaking*, published in 1972.

Satir was very innovative in her approaches and used games, exercises, audio, video, one-way mirrors and demonstrations in her work; approaches which have since become commonplace but were, at that time, novel techniques. She was the first Director of Training at the famous Esalen Institute, in the forefront of the Growth Potential movement. It is said that she was deaf until the age of ten so, like Erickson (*see* below), with some sensory impairment she developed her observation skills to an extraordinarily high degree. Satir died in 1988.

FRITZ (FREDERICK) PERLS

Like Satir, Perls was another of the best-known models for NLP's development. He is often credited as the founder of Gestalt Therapy, although three other people, including his wife, co-authored with him the first book on the subject. Gestalt Psychology dated back to 1912, but Perls turned it into a therapeutic tool. The word 'Gestalt' refers to a pattern of parts which make up a whole and Gestalt Psychology indicates that a study of parts alone is not sufficient to lead to understanding – the whole must be taken into account.

Born in Berlin in 1893, Perls gained an MD in psychiatry. Originally influenced by Freud, he rejected the psychoanalytic movement, believing that the present is more important than the past. Often blunt and ignoring conventional pleasantries, Perls encouraged his subjects to explore their emotional responses through processes including the use of 'hot seats', through which a person could exchange roles by moving to a different seat where they could act out a different part. In 1946 Perls emigrated to the USA, founded the New York Institute for Gestalt Therapy in 1952 and became involved with Esalen, the Californian centre for the human growth movement and associated therapy. He remained there until 1969 when he moved to Canada and founded the Gestalt Institute of British Columbia; six months after it was established, in 1970, he died.

MILTON ERICKSON

Erickson, also part of the trio of notable NLP role models, was born in 1901 in Aurum, Nevada. His parents were pioneers who travelled to their destination in a covered wagon. He was colour blind, perceiving the colour purple, but little else. He was also tone deaf, dyslectic and had arrhythmia – an irregularity of the heart. He did not learn to speak until the age of four and, because of his breathing and hearing, had an unusual vocal pattern. He had two bouts of polio, the first at 17 years of age and the second when he was 51. Although he recovered almost completely from the total paralysis of the first bout, the second left him severely paralysed and in frequent pain, which he alleviated with daily hypnosis exercises.

Erickson completed his MD degree in 1928 and became Chief Psychiatrist at Worcester State Hospital in Massachusetts. He later became Director of Psychiatric Research and Psychiatric Training at Eloise Hospital and Infirmary in Eloise, Michigan, and took on professorships at other centres. In 1948 he moved to Phoenix, Arizona, mainly for health reasons, where he established a private practice and used his hypnotherapy skills to achieve extraordinary results. Later, he became founding President of the American Society of Clinical Hypnosis and founding Editor of the *American Journal of Clinical Hypnosis*.

In later life, Erickson's fame spread and, in his seventies, he was publicly recognized for the hypnosis work for which, in earlier years, he had been condemned by the medical establishment. As one of the subjects of Bandler's and

Grinder's studies, Erickson provided the basis for much of what is now known as the Milton Model in NLP, when his language and behaviour were examined in detail and many patterns defined of which, apparently, he himself had not always consciously been aware. He made particular use of indirect language patterns and ways of gaining rapport with his clients. After two marriages and fathering eight children, Erickson died in March 1980.

FRANK FARRELLY

A psychotherapist, trainer and author and reported to have been involved with the Palo Alto Project, Farrelly is the developer of provocative therapy, which aims to bring about personal change through challenge and humour and, with Jeff Brandsma, author of the book *Provocative Therapy*. He is funny, outrageous, irreverent and almost impossibly direct, while retaining a respect for the subjects of his repartee. He has undoubtedly been a major role model for other well-known NLP figures, although his work is not specifically NLP-based; Richard Bandler apparently visited Farrelly in California and videoed his workshops for later study.

Farrelly's activities have included being Clinical Professor at the School of Social Work at the University of Wisconsin. His interests also include parapsychology, a subject on which he has carried out research and about which he has many fascinating stories to tell.

JUDITH DELOZIER

DeLozier's background was in religious studies and anthropology; she was also a music and dance teacher. Her involvement with NLP started when John Grinder, to whom she was married for some years, gave her a manuscript copy of *The Structure of Magic* to read and comment on. She became one of the co-founders of NLP and originated much of the early NLP material; she was also, with John Grinder, co-developer of New Code NLP. She was introduced to hypnosis work when Gregory Bateson suggested that she work with

Milton Erickson for a time. She specializes in epistemology (the theory of knowledge/study of how people know what they know) and cross-cultural applications of NLP.

LESLIE CAMERON BANDLER

Cameron Bandler was a student of community studies (for which Santa Cruz was famous) and psychology. She was involved with the NLP group at the university and later became the first Research Director of the Society of NLP, set up by Bandler and Grinder. Married to Richard Bandler for a short time (John Grinder conducted the ceremony), she later married Michael Lebeau and, together with Lebeau and David Gordon, she set up an organization in San Rafael, California, called the Centre for Advanced Studies. Cameron Bandler left the NLP world in the mid- to -late 1980s and became very involved in green campaigning in the USA.

DAVID GORDON

A psychology student and one of the original group of co-developers of NLP, Gordon's approach is characterized by curiosity, humour and systematic thinking. His training makes liberal use of metaphor, the subject of a master's degree thesis and, subsequently, one of his best known books, *Therapeutic Metaphors*. He has made major contributions to the field of NLP including, with Cameron Bandler and Lebeau, exploring the structure of subjective experience, developing the Mental Aptitude Patterning (MAP) model and also the Imperative Self, a model which demonstrates what it is about a person which holds constant across contexts and time and is likely to be true from birth to death. Gordon was also the developer, with Graham Dawes, of the Experiential Array, possibly the least publicized major model of NLP!

ROBERT DILTS

Another of the early co-developers of NLP, Dilts was a student at Santa Cruz and also studied with Bateson and

Erickson. He is noted for his creative approach to NLP and for the continuing development of numerous models, the best known being the Neurological Levels model. Fascinated by the study of people who excel in their fields, Dilts wrote a series of books on famous individuals, including Einstein, Walt Disney, Aristotle and Mozart. He also co-authored, with Grinder, Bandler and DeLozier the standard NLP work, *Neuro-Linguistic Programming*, Volume 1. Other interests of his are NLP and spirituality and NLP and health, and he has told of his work with his mother, who had cancer and later made a full recovery. Dilts was also creator of what is probably the first degree course in NLP when he designed his own personal programme which he called Human Engineering.

STEVE AND CONNIRAE ANDREAS

Steve Andreas's mother was Barry Stevens, who was a major figure in the Gestalt world and had a close relationship with Fritz Perls. He lectured in Gestalt and related subjects at the University of Utah, and edited the US magazine *Gestalt Now*. In 1978, he gave up his Gestalt therapy to work with NLP, and is the author, or co-author, of many books on the subject.

Connirae was one of Andreas's students, best known for her work on Core Transformation. She was responsible for tape recording many of Bandler's and Grinder's workshops and, together with Steve, turning them into some of the best-known NLP books around: *Frogs into Princes*, *Trance-formations* and *Re-framing*. They also wrote *Heart of the Mind* and have been active in developing new NLP change patterns and models of human excellence.

TODD EPSTEIN

Epstein became involved in NLP in 1979, having served his apprenticeship with Bandler. He was a partner at the Dynamic Learning Centre and the NLP University, a US training organization, with Dilts and DeLozier. He co-authored several books with Dilts and worked closely with him on developing various NLP models. A great musician, and famous for his story telling abilities, Epstein died in 1995.

TERRENCE MCCLENDON

McClendon was a student at the University of Santa Cruz at the same time as Bandler and Grinder and participated in many of the early NLP group activities. He has a master's degree in psychology and is a licensed counsellor. He is author of *The Wild Days*, a highly personal account of NLP's emergence in California. He went to Australia in the 1970s and founded the Australian Institute of NLP.

STEPHEN GILLIGAN

Gilligan is an internationally recognized authority on Ericksonian therapy, a trainer and therapist. He studied with Bateson at the University of Santa Cruz and was involved in the conception of NLP, but left the field in 1977 when he considered it was becoming 'arrogant and fundamentalist – emphasizing techniques and evidences of programming rather than the meaning of our experience'. His approach, 'Self-relations', concentrates on relationships between the conscious and unconscious minds. Attempting to model Erickson, Gilligan apparently confined himself to a wheelchair, but abandoned this when Erickson feared he would develop unwanted symptoms and persuaded him to simply copy what he did, rather than who he was!

WYATT WOODSMALL

Woodsmall is a business consultant and management trainer. He was co-founder and President of the International NLP Trainer's Association (INLPTA) and the International NLP Business Alliance and President of the North American Association for NLP. He is best known for his work on behavioural modelling. He is also a Senior Vice-president of the International Research Institute for Human Typological Studies, where his main emphasis is on the connection between human differences and performance. With Tad James, one of his students, he wrote *Time Line Therapy*; time line work is a major feature of NLP (*see* chapter 3) and with

Marvin Oka, he then extended time line work into *Time Codes*.

TAD JAMES

James has a master's degree in communications, a PhD in Ericksonian Hypnosis and was originally a business consultant. He is probably best known for work with time lines and is co-creator, with Woodsmall, of Time Line Therapy, a specific approach to resolving problems using hypnotic techniques in association with mental 'movement through time'. He also specializes in another, rather esoteric, doctrine, Hawaiian Huna, an ancient spiritual tradition which has become increasingly used in recent years. He has also run courses in Mesmerism, an almost forgotten, and often misunderstood, precursor to modern-day hypnosis.

CHARLES FAULKNER

Faulkner studied with the original developers of NLP, his own field at that time being literature. He applies NLP and cognitive science to business and is the principal co-author of the audio programmes *NLP: The New Technology of Achievement* and *Success Mastery with NLP* as well as co-author, with Steve Andreas, of the book *NLP: The New Technology of Achievement*.

CHRISTINA HALL

Hall is best known for her work on new patterns and concepts in language. In 1981, Bandler invited her to train with him, which she did for six years. Hall's research interests include exploring language production as a powerful catalyst of change.

ANTHONY ROBBINS

Robbins has probably done more to popularize NLP than anyone. An American, he injects as much energy into his presentations as a whole army of conventional trainers, and at 6ft 7in is a larger than life figure. An ex-salesman, he is famous for his large-scale events (involving several thousand people), at which he talks about sales, leadership and enhancing personal potential. Robbins has produced many popular books and audiotapes about using NLP, the best known probably being his 1987 book *Unlimited Power*. As a high spot of the final day of his courses, participants are encouraged to walk on hot coals, on the premise that if they can gain the personal confidence to do this, they can do anything!

GENE EARLY

Apparently the first person to give workshops on NLP in Europe, Early was one of the founders of the UKTC in Great Britain. He had a background in Transactional Analysis (TA) therapy, trained with Bandler and Grinder and later became a Vice-Chancellor of the University of the Nations in Hawaii, a Christian missions organization.

GRAHAM DAWES

A British trainer and founder Director of the UKTC, Dawes came across NLP when doing a BA by independent study as a mature student and, with the encouragement of his tutor and colleague, Ian Cunningham, made it the focus of his degree. He works closely with Gordon, especially in their development of Experiential Dynamics (*see* chapter 3).

IAN CUNNINGHAM, ROY JOHNSON, DAVID GASTER AND BARBARA WITNEY

Other trainers who were instrumental in the early development of NLP in the UK. Cunningham did a lot of early training at the UKTC and was the developer of self-managed learning. Gaster was well known in the USA and UK and was a flyer with the Red Arrows. Johnson was involved in many early NLP programmes and Witney was another regular US trainer with UKTC in its early days.

ERIC JENSEN

Jensen is a leading writer and practitioner of accelerated learning. Having trained with Bandler in the mid-1970s, he became interested in how the use of different senses impinged on the learning process and his first book, *Super Teaching*, utilized NLP techniques in conjunction with teaching theory.

SHELLE ROSE CHARVET

Charvet, a Canadian, trained with Rodger Bailey, the developer of the Language and Behaviour (LAB) profile (a questionnaire which identifies people's use of NLP meta-programmes). She is the author of *Words that Change Minds*, an excellent book on the use of meta-programmes in influencing.

DAVID GROVE

Grove helps people explore how they use metaphor and metaphorical space around themselves, through his process of cognitive mapping. He has also developed the concept of 'clean language' – a way of using entirely neutral language in order to avoid imposing the therapist's own perceptions upon the client.

This chapter has outlined the activities of several of the people who have been most influential in NLP. There are many more who cannot be mentioned here because of lack of space but, for those interested, there is a wealth of further reading available, as well as the opportunity to attend workshops and training events at which some of these people present their ideas and work.

3 • FRAMEWORKS, MODELS AND TECHNIQUES

Over the years, there has been a divergence of opinion about what constitutes NLP. For those not familiar with the field, NLP can seem like a collection of techniques and processes which, if used effectively, can produce extraordinary results. The popular press, in particular, have focused on those NLP processes which sound unusual or extraordinary which has often given the impression that NLP is quirky and just a collection of 'quick fixes'. However, it is much more than its component parts; providing a holistic and broad approach to the development of excellence, which is not always apparent to those who concentrate exclusively on its specific and characteristic 'technology'.

Having said the subject is more than its parts, however, for those interested in how NLP enables people to achieve success, this chapter is devoted to outlining and exploring the frameworks, models and techniques which give NLP its particular character. Frameworks and models are not complete explanations of reality, but they do act as helpful guides to how people function. Techniques cannot be used in isolation; they may be helpful, but need to be set in the context of the whole person

and the whole situation. The breakdown into the different cat-
egories is somewhat arbitrary; I have chosen to group the
broader conceptual approaches as frameworks, the more spe-
cific ones as models and the ones with detailed practical
applications as techniques, which I hope makes it relatively
easy to follow.

FRAMEWORKS

EXPERIENTIAL ARRAY

The Experiential Array was developed by David Gordon
(USA) and Graham Dawes (UK) as a joint project, beginning
in 1987 and being refined, especially in the area of 'beliefs'
until the present day. The array creates a framework for
exploring the structure of effective performance and is, I
believe, the simplest way of understanding what NLP can
offer.

In essence, the array has two applications: personal
change, and modelling and performance enhancement.

It outlines five elements which contribute to performance:

- outcomes
- behaviour
- mental strategies
- emotions
- beliefs

Each of these interrelates so the whole forms a complete system, with the 'internal' elements of thinking and feeling
affecting 'external' behaviour, and behaviour affecting the
results (outcomes) achieved. Because of these interrelationships, if one part of the system changes, it has an effect on
others, creating changes in them also.

The diagram overleaf represents the interrelations of these
elements and also indicates the degrees of influence exerted
by them on each other. So the relative size of the arrows indicates the degree of influence, with the impact of feelings and
thoughts on behaviour having a greater effect than the impact

of behaviour on feeling and thinking. Similarly, beliefs have a greater impact on thoughts, feeling and behaviour than any of these have on beliefs at any given time. Over time, of course, these elements may contribute experiences which ultimately change beliefs.

The Experiential Array

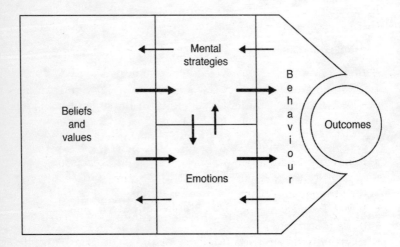

As context is important, the five elements described above may vary from situation to situation. For example, a person may have one kind of behaviour at work (one context) and a different kind of behaviour at home (different context). Also, within the same context, different individuals may have widely different patterns of thoughts, feelings and behaviour and aim for different objectives.

So this framework illustrates the process by which a person achieves results in a particular area. If a different result (outcome) is desired, then something needs to be changed within the system. In looking at the array, it is easy to see why a saying popular in NLP is true: 'If you always do what you've always done, you always get what you've always got!' The framework shows how, if we utilize the same ways of thinking and acting, we get the same results, and also shows that, if we make changes in these areas, we can develop and progress.

NEUROLOGICAL LEVELS (SOMETIMES CALLED LOGICAL LEVELS)

This very well-known approach to NLP was developed by Robert Dilts. The framework helps in thinking about learning, change and personal development and was inspired by Gregory Bateson, who identified four levels of learning and change, with each level 'more abstract than the level below it but each having a greater degree of impact on the individual' (Dilts).

This framework has six basic levels at which an individual can be 'operating'; in ascending order they are:

- environment (where and when things happen; opportunities and constraints)
- behaviour (what a person does; actions and reactions)
- capability (how a person does things, the skills utilized; the strategy and plans followed)
- belief (why a person does things and what that person finds motivating)
- identity (who a person thinks he or she is; the sense of self and personal mission)
- spirituality (what a person does things for, including family and community; what exists beyond herself)

These levels are considered as a hierarchy, with spirituality at the top and environment at the bottom, each level 'involving more of an individual's neurology'. The levels are sometimes depicted as nested circles but more often as triangles, with the first five levels as the base triangle and the higher levels as an inverted triangle above (*see* diagram overleaf).

The framework can be used in a variety of ways; one being to check for consistency (congruence) between each level. For example, a person might think it important to be on time for meetings but in practice often be late. So the belief

43

(timeliness is important) is contradicted by the behaviour (lateness). The framework helps people check whether what they think and do lines up with their self-identity and values; inconsistency or conflict between these areas can lead to stress, misunderstanding by others and poor performance.

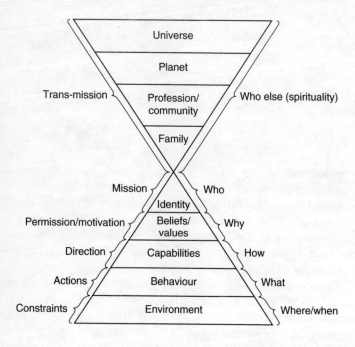

The framework can also be applied to organizations. If a consultant is called into a company to advise on customer care, questions relating to the Neurological Levels framework can help identify any inconsistencies in what is happening. For example, the workplace may give an impression of untidiness, and staff may not listen well to customers' views; both of these could be at odds with an organizational belief that paying attention to the customer is important. It may also be the case that the staff's beliefs about customer care do not correspond with those of the organization, leading to mixed messages being given to those who visit it.

TIME LINES

This is a conceptual framework which deals with how people perceive themselves in relation to time and shows that people store time-based information in different ways.

The idea of time lines goes back a long way; it was familiar to the ancient Greeks and has featured in thinking and writing over the centuries. In 1890, psychologist William James, writing in *Principles of Psychology*, referred to the concept of time having locations; Tad James (*see* chapter 2) has referred to William James as saying that 'the present is a saddle-back on which we sit perched, and we look in two directions in time; location in space corresponds to time. We date a memory simply by tossing it in a certain direction.'

Time Line theory involves the concept that people 'organize' time in different ways and react to time in different ways. To take a simple example, time often goes slowly when it seems uncontrollable (for example while waiting in a traffic jam) and passes rapidly during enjoyable events. Time therefore is not a fixed concept, but one which varies according to our perception of it. NLP takes the concept of time further and makes it possible to imagine ourselves at different points in time and at different 'places' in relation to it.

To illustrate, let us take the concept of moving through time. It is possible to imagine a line on the floor, one end of which represents the past and the other the future; the present time is somewhere between. It is then possible to stand on the line at the spot which equates to the present time, look towards the future and imagine how it could be (for example seeing oneself carrying out a particular activity or having achieved a particular result). It is also possible to look back at the past in the same way to recall how one behaved then. Doing this visualization can help clarify one's feelings about certain events and occurrences. It is also possible to move physically along the line as if one were revisiting the past or moving into the future. From these points it becomes relatively easy to access or reaccess the feelings which relate to the events concerned. Once immersed in these events, it is possible to evaluate them from a different standpoint (literally) and learn about one's responses and make appropriate changes.

The concept of time lines, really a metaphorical way of working with the topic, provides an excellent method of working through issues, getting different perspectives and developing greater personal control.

UNIFIED FIELD THEORY

Many people have thought about ways of integrating the whole field of NLP into one framework. Robert Dilts has produced one such framework. He says that Albert Einstein '. . . sought a "unified field theory" for physics, which would tie together all physical theories into a single model of how the universe operated'; he also says, 'Neuro-Linguistic Programming began as a unified field theory – an operational framework that synthesized the fields of neurology, linguistics and artificial intelligence.'

Dilts says that, as NLP progressed, it moved away from the systemic model and towards linear 'step-by-step' approaches. He believes that, although this has led to rapid transfer of skills and techniques, it has resulted in the loss of a 'bigger picture', so that many students of NLP struggle to understand how the tools and techniques they have learned fit together.

In order to overcome this, he has devised a framework for understanding human performance; the framework has three elements:

- levels of functioning
- time
- perspective

On one level this framework is about how all the techniques of NLP fit together and on another level it is about the relationships between NLP and other systems of thought. The framework also addresses generative processes, ie ones which promote evolution and growth. Dilts says:

> Generative NLP helps people solve problems and achieve goals in a more systemic and organic way. When new

46

resources are created and developed, problems that are ready to be solved by those resources emerge and resolve naturally and without effort.

Dilts's integrating framework helps people 'develop elegance in managing the multiple levels and multiple perspectives of change and communication'. By learning how to operate within multidimensional 'spaces', people can achieve objectives through selecting the most appropriate courses of action to take. The diagram below shows how Dilts has conceived inter-relationships between the three elements.

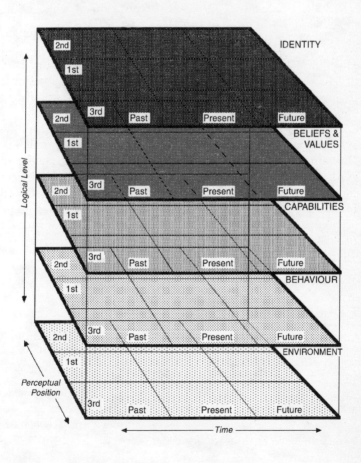

These elements have also been referred to as the 'Jungle Gym' and shown diagrammatically as a matrix with various 'boxes' (it has also, apparently, been built as a climbing frame which can be used in a physical way to explore the connections and experiences involved).

NEW CODE NLP

New Code is a holistic way of approaching human potential and the book *Turtles All the Way Down* by Grinder and DeLozier, written in 1987, is an exposition of some of its ideas. New Code grew out of the work of Carlos Castaneda and Gregory Bateson as well as Grinder and DeLozier's experience of Native American Indians, African drumming, dancing, singing, story-telling and anthropological studies. Some of its approaches include active dreaming, the development of intuition and what are called 'personal edits', designed to integrate elements of brain activity.

Part of New Code is about the body's own ability to act as a feedback mechanism and the New Code approach teaches that the body has its own inborn wisdom and that, by listening to the body, it is possible to obtain excellent information about what is, or is not, appropriate action to take.

New Code has not been outlined in a structured way (perhaps because its very approach assumes an integrated and holistic way of functioning). The best description of New Code may be found in a transcript of a talk given by Judith DeLozier in 1993, in London, the main elements of which were printed in the Swiss periodical *NLP World* in 1995. The following paragraphs are a summary of this presentation.

'Old coding', or traditional NLP, arose from linguistics, Gestalt Therapy and systems theory. These disciplines produced the NLP language patterns and showed how they connected with the deep structure of experience. The ideas of representational systems, sub-modalities, strategies, separating intent from behaviour and many other NLP techniques followed. Connections were made between the patterns of physiology, language and internal state. So traditional NLP explored structures of experience, the ways in which these structures are expressed in language and techniques for analysing and working with people's personal experience.

However, according to DeLozier, people were viewing NLP as technology, as a procedure – or, in her words, a ritual. She and Grinder felt there was no 'wisdom' in the technology itself, but that it had to reside in the person who was undertaking the change processes. New Code NLP provided a way for the inherent wisdom of the body to be acknowledged and utilized and Grinder and DeLozier defined New Code as containing the following elements:

1 **State**. This is about developing an appropriate state in which to enhance excellence. One of the elements here is what Castaneda called 'stopping the world', a very clear state where internal dialogue is turned off, vision shifted from the centre to the periphery, and tension allowed to dissipate.

2 **Conscious–unconscious relationship**. This is about having a highly developed quality relationship between conscious and unconscious resources, knowing when to use the 'tight thinking of the cognitive conscious mind' and when to use the 'loose thinking of the more creative unconscious mind'. This is also to do with perceptual positions and the ability to shift in and out of detached perspectives on oneself.

3 **Balance between practice and spontaneity**. This is about allowing oneself to let go of deliberate activity and just 'be'. For example in the martial art Aikido, after practising and practising, there comes a time when you just act – not deliberating what to do, but just doing.

4 **Perceptual position**. Shifting positions allows us different perspectives on a situation. If you imagine watching yourself interacting with another person, you can begin to understand the part you both play in maintaining the interaction and what you could do to enhance it.

5 **Attention**. Where you place your attention defines the quality of your perception; by paying tightly focused attention to one aspect, you may ignore others. If you find that

fixing your attention on one aspect of an interaction leads you to a negative value judgment, you may choose to move your attention to another part and thereby notice if the quality of the interaction becomes more positive.

6 **Filters**. Everyone perceives things selectively, according to their experience and conditioning. By asking what filters you can let go of, you can push back your personal boundaries and experience even more.

7 **Multiple descriptions**. This is about widening our range of definitions, so instead of having just one approach to an issue, we can broaden our response to it.

SYSTEMIC NLP

Although not a single discrete framework, the systemic approach to NLP is concerned with relationships and interactions. Instead of isolating component parts of a system and looking at them as discrete units, the systemic approach shows how the whole can become more than the sum of its parts and how one part of a system can impinge on, and interact with, another. Robert Dilts says of both New Code and Systemic NLP that they:

> . . . were both developed in order to refocus NLP back onto its original roots. Their purpose has been to help NLP become more 'code congruent' with its presuppositions and the legacy of those individuals who served as its initial role models. The mission of systemic NLP and NLP New Coding is to reintroduce a cybernetic framework and bring systemic thinking skills into the practice of NLP.

MODELS

A model may be described as a representation of a system or process; a representation which shows the component parts and how they interrelate. 'Modelling' is a term much used in NLP, and it has a number of possible definitions. Probably the most common description of the term is as a process whereby someone either analyses or copies (or both) another person's ways, or patterns of behaving, thinking or reacting.

For example, you might find that one neighbour always cuts the grass by walking up and down in straight lines while another moves in decreasing circles; you could then copy each in turn and see what results you get.

There are two different types of modelling within NLP. The first is what can be termed Deep Trance Identification. This is carried out by 'absorbing' another person's characteristics by spending time immersed in observation and assimilation of their behaviour. The word 'trance' is used because the state in which this absorption of the other person's behaviour takes place is one of total focus (often in an 'unconscious' manner) on the subject.

The second kind of modelling is called Strategy Modelling. This process (first presented to the world in the book *Neuro-Linguistic Programming*, Volume 1), involves a conscious exploration of the elements involved in a person's performance. The Experiential Dynamics framework (see 'Experiential Array' above) utilizes this process. With strategy modelling, it is possible to analyse and codify an individual's objectives, behaviour and ways of thinking and feeling; this analysis can be as detailed as required including, for example, tiny sub-elements of thinking (sub-modalities) such as the size and shape of images people visualize, the precise locations of feelings in their body and the precise breakdown of their behaviour, such as the position they sit in while making a telephone call or the colour ink they select to sign their letters. It is worth remembering that, in modelling, the most elegant approach is to model simply the elements which make the *difference* between average performance and excellent performance; it is not necessary to model absolutely everything the person being modelled does.

WELL FORMED OUTCOMES

NLP has a model dealing with objective setting, called the 'Well Formed Outcomes' model (WFO for short). It is a starting point for most NLP work as the definition of a clear and achievable desired result is the key to achievement. For more details of this model, *see* chapters 1 and 6.

TOTE

This model was developed by George Miller, Eugene Galanter and Karl Pribram and was first proposed in their book *Plans and the Structure of Behaviour* in 1960. It shows a feedback mechanism, which can be used as an aid to problem solving, creativity and development.

Feedback mechanisms are very common in automated processes and NLP applies the concept to behaviour, showing that, if we are not achieving a desired result, we need to take further action in order to succeed.

The TOTE has three elements:

- T = test
- O = operate
- E = exit

If we take the example of starting a car, the engine needs to be switched on before the car can move. The 'test' is 'Is the engine switched on?'. If it is, the car starts and the person can 'exit' from that procedure. If the engine is not switched on, something needs to happen – an 'operation'. By turning the key, the engine starts. The 'test' can then be repeated, 'Is the engine switched on?' The answer this time is 'Yes' and so the person can now exit.

The process assumes a goal, or outcome, and a variety of ways of achieving that goal. By trying out different approaches, the goal can be reached.

Translating the TOTE to interpersonal relations, a typical process could be as follows:

'Is the shop assistant being helpful to me?' (test)
'No' (therefore no exit)
'What could I do differently? How about smiling?' (operate)
'Is the assistant being helpful now?' (test again)
'Yes' (OK, exit)

The TOTE helps people evaluate what they are doing and be more flexible in order to achieve good results. The diagram opposite shows this process in action.

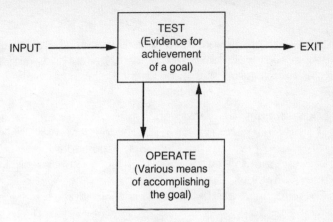

The cycle of 'Test → Operate' can be conducted as many times as necessary in order to achieve the result.

ROLE

Developed by Robert Dilts, ROLE helps identify how people think – and consequently behave; it covers four factors:

- R = representational systems (Which of the senses – sight, sound, touch, taste, smell – does the person use most for the particular stage in their thinking?)
- O = orientation (Is the person orientated internally – towards memories or imagination – or externally – towards the outside world?)
- L = linkage (How is one step in the strategy linked to the others in a sequence – do different stages overlap or are they sequential stages?)
- E = effect (What is the effect, result or purpose of the step in the strategy – for example, to access, organize, evaluate or judge information?)

By considering each of these elements, it is possible to map a person's thought experience to enhance creativity and effectiveness.

SCORE

This model, developed by Robert Dilts and Todd Epstein between 1987 and 1991, has to do with creative problem solving and suggests that there are five elements involved in this process. These elements are:

- S = symptoms ('the most noticeable and conscious aspects of a problem state; remaining fairly constant over time')
- C = causes ('underlying elements responsible for creating and maintaining symptoms; tending to be less obvious than symptoms')
- O = outcomes ('desired states or goals that take the place of symptoms')
- R = resources ('elements responsible for transforming causes and symptoms and creating and maintaining outcomes or effects')
- E = effects ('responses to, or results of, achieving an outcome; they may be positive or negative in how they affect motivation')

The five elements interrelate and can be assessed and handled in different ways in order to achieve solutions.

LANGUAGE MODELS

There are a range of language models in NLP; the best known are probably the Meta-Model and the Milton Model.

The **Meta-Model** was developed by Richard Bandler and John Grinder. It is so called because it is about one representation (words) being used to explore another representation (experience) which is beyond the words themselves. It is grounded in the work of earlier linguists, such as Chomsky and Korzybski (*see* chapter 2) and indicates that language is an external demonstration of internal experience and that it has structure, with words forming a 'surface' structure, representing 'deep structure' or experience itself. Language is not reality, it simply represents reality and understanding the meaning of someone's language helps in understanding that person's actual experience, which is beyond the words themselves.

The model considers three factors which can produce confusion and misunderstanding:

- deletion
- distortion
- generalization

In other words, people do not always say exactly, or completely, what they mean, but leave things out, change them or turn them into broad categories rather than specific points. If you were to say, 'I always enjoy going out with friends', the statement sounds quite specific. However, there may be some places you do not like going with friends (for example to events they like and you do not); there may be some friends you like seeing for short times, but get bored with quickly on outings; there may be some times when you actually dislike going out with friends (for example when there is the last part of a riveting serial on television). So your statement is not invariably true or actually factually correct; it is a broad statement of your attitude towards an activity.

Now this is actually a good thing, for absolute precision can lead to pedantic and interminable conversations. The Meta-Model, however, allows us to question communications in the furtherance of better understanding. Some examples of how the model does this are as follows:

Statement: I did very well in the exams.
Meta-Model question: What do you mean by 'very well'?
Aim: To clarify the level of performance.

Statement: It's bad to be late.
Meta-Model question: Who says so?
Aim: To find where the person's beliefs about lateness came from.

Statement: Everyone has problems with public speaking.
Meta-Model question: Absolutely everyone?
Aim: To show the statement is a generalization and allow the person to rethink.

So the Meta-Model is concerned with precision, clarity and mutual understanding. A fuller exposition is provided in *The Structure of Magic*, Volume 1, the original work which presented the Meta-Model to the world (see also *Precision* by Michael McMaster and John Grinder).

The **Milton Model** is also concerned with language and is, in many ways, the converse of the Meta-Model. The Milton Model is based on the language patterns of Milton Erickson (*see* chapter 2). While the Meta-Model is concerned with precision and clarity, the Milton Model is concerned with indirect and general language used to influence.

Milton Erickson was a master of communication, using language creatively and flexibly to achieve results with his patients. Although some people have said he was not always consciously aware of the processes he was using, when studied by Bandler and Grinder distinctive patterns emerged in what he did. Some of these patterns were codified and are now known as the Milton Model, some features of which are generalization, ambiguity, indirect language and suggestion. In considering the Meta-Model above, we found that its purpose was clarity and precision, so why is there a place for the direct opposite of this? The answer is that sometimes being non-specific allows for the use of the imagination, which can lead to creative thought and accessing of the unconscious mind. The use of suggestion can also lead to change in a non-directive manner.

Let us take an example to illustrate these two points. Suppose a friend asks your advice on buying clothes. Knowing she often selects inappropriate garments, you might use Milton Model language to help her, while not being too prescriptive. You might say something along the following lines (the words in bold are indirect suggestions and the words in bold capitals are non-specific words): 'You might like to **consider** something **DRAMATIC**; possibly a **BRIGHTER** colour than you usually wear, with a **BOLD** design. You could **think about something different**, and maybe **go to a new designer** whose clothes are **RIGHT FOR YOUR LIFE STYLE**.'

There are many more elements to the Milton Model and we will take one final one here. This is the use of language to shift a person's thinking into different time frames. This might include taking him back into the past to explore or gain a different perspective on events which have occurred. Probably a more common use, however, is that of shifting someone (metaphorically) by using the future tense. So, if a person is finding it difficult to start a task, you could say, 'When you have finished that, you will be really pleased and feel good about having completed it.' This implies there will be a time when the task has been completed and also begins to allow the person to create for himself the feeling he will get when the task has been done. A simple shift of language produces a boost to both confidence and motivation.

If you are interested in learning more about the Milton Model, there are many books available, as well as transcripts of Erickson's own work and videos of him in action. Some of these sources are listed in the Bibliography.

THE DISNEY STRATEGY

Finally, here is an example of a model developed from observing one individual. Much of NLP is about role modelling others in order to find out how they get results, and then helping others achieve similar results through transfer of the skills involved. The Disney Strategy is based on Walt Disney and is outlined in the books *Tools for Dreamers* by Robert B Dilts, Todd Epstein and Robert W Dilts, and *Skills for the Future* by Robert Dilts with Gino Bonissone. The strategy is a representation of how Disney achieved some of his creative results.

Dilts says that people were often puzzled by Disney, as he seemed to shift from one way of behaving to another. Dilts codified Disney's behaviour and found it fell into three distinct elements, which he called the 'Dreamer', the 'Realist' and the 'Critic'. The Dreamer 'generates the initial conceptual formulation of the idea'. The Realist 'carries out the task of implementing the idea in a tangible form'. The Critic 'is the evaluator; the one that really turns something into a valuable contribution'.

Each of these 'states' seems to have its own characteristic posture and thought processes. For example the Dreamer can be represented looking up, being relaxed, focusing on the broad picture and thinking that anything is possible; the Realist can be represented looking ahead, leaning forward, considering short-term activities and assuming results are achievable; the Critic can be represented as looking down, asking questions and thinking about what to do if problems occur.

Dilts proposed that using these three states could help in creativity and problem solving and goes on, in his writing, to show how this can be developed further. This model is an excellent exposition of how to do behavioural modelling and provides a useful way of understanding and teaching creative processes.

TECHNIQUES

We can now move to some of the techniques which NLP offers for enhancing awareness, developing flexibility and bringing about change.

PERCEPTUAL POSITIONS

People often use phrases which refer to positions, such as saying, 'If I were in your position' or 'I can see your point of view'. However, it is not always so easy to really understand how another person thinks, feels and acts. Perceptual positions offer ways of making such shifts of perspective.

NLP refers to a whole series of 'perceptual positions'. If a person is 'in first position' she is very much grounded in her own body and often subject to strong emotional feelings. In contrast, being 'in second position' is about being detached and able to observe oneself from a different perspective. NLP calls the experience of being 'in first position' being *associated* and being 'in second position' being *dissociated* as the diagram opposite illustrates.

In the associated state, one's experiences may be heightened. It is possible to relive past experiences 'as if one were still there' and to imagine future experiences in a similar way.

'ASSOCIATED'   'DISSOCIATED'

First position
(where you are now)

Second position
(imagining watching
yourself from a distance)

The disadvantages of being associated are that it may be difficult to manage or critically review one's feelings and one may sometimes feel submerged by emotions; a problem if past traumatic events are very much alive in one's imagination.

In the dissociated state it is possible to adopt a more detached view and be able to monitor what one does as one does it; the disadvantage is that it can cut off emotional responses and give the impression of being cold and distant.

Beyond first and second positions are a series of additional perspectives, called 'Meta-positions' as they relate to positions beyond the original ones. Sometimes the next position ('third position') is called 'a helicopter view' because, in this position, both the individual and any others with whom he is interacting can be observed at the same time. It is possible then to take on additional positions where one is 'watching oneself watching oneself'. Although 'third position' has been called an observer position, one writer (Sinclair) has suggested that, by virtue of observing, the third person is, in effect, part of the situation and not beyond it at all and that true Meta-positions are beyond third position, not just beyond second position.

An example of these positions is shown overleaf where a customer is in a shop waiting to be served.

- In circle 1 the customer queues up to be served (first position).
- In circle 2 an assistant helps the customer (second position).
- In circle 3 another person, behind the customer, waits in line and observes the other two (third position).

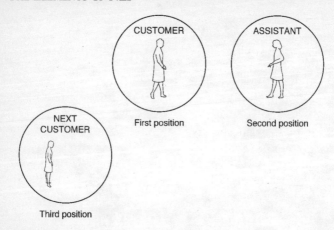

Shifting perspective can aid self-awareness, help understanding of other people's perspectives and make it possible to step back from one's emotions and review them in a more detached manner.

REFRAMING

This technique also deals with shifts of perception.

'Reframing' means simply to put another possible meaning on an event, a thought, a feeling or an act. As an example, a sore throat may be thought of as a nuisance; it could, however, be reframed as an opportunity to rest or a chance to think and solve problems. By thinking of it in a different way, it is possible to be more positive and make the most of the situation.

People can reframe events for themselves or help others to reframe their own thoughts and experiences. Reframing can be used in a variety of contexts, including therapy, business and personal growth.

CHUNKING

This technique, borrowed from information technology, is also, in some ways, about shifts of perspective. By considering a situation from different angles, and at different levels, it is possible to gain insights into how to deal with it.

One way of thinking about a situation is to consider its component parts. The terms used here are 'chunking up' (thinking what lies beyond the issue being considered) and 'chunking down' (thinking what the component parts of an issue are). It is also possible to consider the 'chunks' on either side of an issue; in other words the elements parallel to it (*see* chapter 6 for an illustration of this process).

A further way of thinking about chunking is to consider how a large task or activity can be broken down into small parts ('small chunk') in order to become more manageable. An example often given is: 'You can eat an elephant if you cut it up into small enough bits first.' The process can be reversed and 'large chunks' considered if a person's thinking is being limited by going into unnecessary detail on a topic.

Excellent results can be achieved by helping people consider appropriate chunk sizes in what they are doing. Some applications are time management (take small tasks at a time) and reading (get an overview first – 'large chunk' – then read the small print – 'small chunk').

ANCHORING

This technique is about the management of responses. The technique is grounded in the behaviourist approach to learning which teaches that responses can be 'conditioned' by association. An early example of this approach was Pavlov, whose work with dogs became world famous; the dogs learned to salivate when they heard a bell which had been rung as their food had been provided. Later, the bell alone produced a similar salivatory response. This process is like the experience of hearing a particular tune and finding it brings back a memory, or smelling a particular food and remembering where you were the first time you ate it.

Anchoring involves associating a trigger (or stimulus) with a response. So, for example, touching a person's shoulder when she is smiling can lead her, in the future, to feel good when touched again in a similar way. Similarly a negative tone of voice, used frequently, can trigger the expectation of criticism.

Anchors come in a variety of forms: simple ones such as a touch or a sound and more complex ones involving movement or chains (sequences) of linked anchors, each one leading the person into a further state of emotional response.

Anchoring is useful in helping a person to stay in a positive emotional state (for example calmness or cheerfulness) and can be used to good effect in therapeutic situations.

Richard Bandler has defined anchoring as 'the pairing of a stimuli [sic] with a highly predictable set of responses' (R Bandler and J LeValle, *Persuasion Engineering*, Meta-Publications Inc, 1996).

PARTS

Another technique which can be helpful in understanding confusion, solving problems and resolving conflict is the use of parts. The term 'parts' is really metaphorical, relating to the fact that people often talk as if they were more than one entity. For example a person might say: 'Part of me wants to change jobs, but another part thinks it would be better to stay where I am.'

It is possible to use the concept of parts to help a person come to terms with the differing elements of his personality. One way of doing this is to notice what he does when talking about different parts; often he will gesture in a particular direction when mentioning the different elements. For example he might gesture to the left for one part and to the right for another; it is then possible to work with this representation and talk as if the parts were embodied and actually visible to the left or right and, if appropriate, get the person to say what size and shape each part is, what they look like, how they move, how they sound and so forth.

By treating the parts as if they have individual personalities it is possible then to work with them as if they were real, helping the person to understand what the roles of the parts are and how they can be utilized or overcome. Again, many of the applications of parts work are in therapy.

SUB-MODALITIES

'Sub-modalities' is the term given to the distinctions made between aspects of sensory awareness. Five senses are generally recognized: sight, hearing, touch, taste and smell. In addition, some writers have identified what they believe is a further sense, that of balance and equilibrium, governed by the vestibular system in the body. (For an account of this see *Leaves Before the Wind* and *Rapport*, Issue 18) NLP works with each of these and helps people to make distinctions between how they perceive the detail of each of the senses.

For example, take the sense of sight. You can actually see things or you can imagine them in your mind; ie mentally visualize them. The mental sub-modalities of sight include:

- distance (are you imagining things close to yourself or far away?)
- brightness (do you have a bright image or a dull one?)
- colour (do you have a black and white picture in your mind or a coloured one?)
- movement (do you see pictures as if they were photographs or as if they were movie films?)
- size (do you imagine large or small images?)
- self-perception (do you see yourself in your images or not?)

Sub-modalities of sound can include loudness, pitch, speed, tonality, closeness, direction and so forth. Part of hearing is sensing external sounds and part is imagining your own voice or other sounds in your head.

Sub-modalities of touch can include warmth, texture and tingling. Also included in this category is non-tactile feeling (ie emotional responses) including, for example, calmness, enthusiasm, sadness, energy, etc. Sub-modalities of taste include sweetness, sourness and bitterness, and sub-modalities of smell include acrid and sweet.

So each of the senses has its subdivisions and a major feature of NLP is its ability to help people make fine distinctions between elements and then manipulate these elements in their imagination to create new and effective experiences. For example, a person who wished to change job could be helped to imagine a range of possibilities; perhaps working in a particular environment or with new skills. The experience would be 'brought to life' by helping the person make mental impressions of the new situations and then modifying them to check their appeal. To take one small example, she might be encouraged to picture herself in a new situation – perhaps running a meeting or presenting a new idea to a work team. She could then be helped to make her mental experience 'bigger' by making the images brighter and closer and the sounds louder and more lively. She could then check whether she found this appealing or daunting. NLP makes this kind of mental manoeuvring a useful tool for those contemplating change.

Because of the power of the mind, sub-modality changes can bring about major shifts in thinking and feeling, with resultant effects in behavioural terms, and we will be exploring this further in section 2 of this book.

SENSORY PREFERENCES

This is an area for which NLP is noted, yet it is really a small part of what NLP can offer. Individual people vary in the use they make of the different senses. Some are very visual, others are more auditory (concerned with language, sounds and 'internal dialogue'); others kinaesthetic (relying heavily on their feelings). Some people use their senses of taste (gustatory) and smell (olfactory) to a high degree.

NLP has recognized that people often use specific words when using different sensory channels (for example a visual person might use phrases such as 'I see', 'I can picture that', 'It looks good', while a kinaesthetic person might say 'I feel weighed down by that' 'It's a bit deep for me', 'Run that past me again', and an auditory person might say 'It sounds good', 'That strikes a chord' and a person using internal dialogue a lot might say 'I think that's a good idea', 'It's in my mind to agree').

In order to tell which sensory channels people are using, NLP suggests that elements such as eye movements and speed of speech can be helpful. For example, people often look up to visualize and look down when they are immersed in strong feelings. Similarly, people tend to speak quickly when visualizing, as their speech is having to keep up with rapidly produced mental images, whereas people who are experiencing feelings tend to speak slowly as feelings are often slow to access.

There are many applications for sensory awareness; for example Robert Dilts has developed a strategy for teaching spelling which relies on the use of visualization and kinaesthetic checks to assist in the process of perceiving and remembering the structure of words.

RAPPORT

Another area for which NLP is well known is helping people create and maintain good relationships. Developing rapport is a vital step in relating to others effectively and there are some very specific NLP techniques for achieving this, which we will be discussing in chapter 5.

FUTURE PACING/NEW BEHAVIOUR GENERATION

Future pacing is the process whereby a person imagines doing something in the future in order to check what the results might be; an invaluable aid to decision making. One particular application of future pacing is the New Behaviour Generator, developed by Leslie Cameron Bandler, which uses a combination of role modelling and future pacing to first imagine, and then mentally experience, a new way of acting. *See* chapters 4 and 6 for more on these techniques.

SWISH/FAST PHOBIA CURES AND PERSPECTIVE PATTERNS

These techniques offer rapid ways of helping people change their perception of a situation; they rely on alterations in how the mind perceives reality although obvious precursors exist the swish process has been attributed to Richard Bandler, the fast phobia cure to Bandler and Grinder, and perspective patterns were developed by John McWhirter.

Swish and perspective pattern techniques may utilize various senses in order to bring about shifts of perception (in this, there is also a similarity to DHE – *see* 'Development in NLP' below). For example a positive mental image may be superimposed on a negative one in order to reprogramme the mind to respond in a positive way to a situation. Alternatively, positive sounds or dialogue may be substituted for negative ones, or compared with negative ones in order to put them in perspective. The actual techniques for doing this in therapy can vary, according to the process the individual therapist considers appropriate.

Approaches to phobias include helping people to experience situations in a detached way. This may involve imagining watching themselves in a situation rather than reliving the actual experience, or imagining the situation as if it were being experienced by someone else (a perceptual shift). Other ways of helping people deal with phobias include using approaches which bring some novelty to the situation; for example making it seem humorous, exaggerating elements of it or altering the person's perception of time so that it is experienced as speeded up, slowed down or reversed.

Such techniques give people ways of becoming more positive and overcoming problems but, as they offer very powerful ways of working with difficult or traumatic events, they do need to be used under supervision.

DEVELOPMENTS IN NLP

As NLP has progressed, there have been many new and associated developments. New Code NLP, mentioned above, was one of these. Another development has been Design Human Engineering (DHE), created by Richard Bandler. This includes elements such as mental 'control panels', to help people alter their personal experiences (including pain control) and the use of external sounds (possibly music, animals or other people speaking) to remove negative self criticism by substituting more positive mental patterns. With this approach, the way the new patterns are installed is important in the success of the processes. Other developments include Tad James's Time

Line Therapy (a way of taking a person back in time, in a trance state, to identify and neutralize emotional traumas), Judith DeLozier's Somatic Syntax (using the fact that body movements have structure, rather like sentences, and utilizing this awareness to enhance actions and interactions), John McWhirter's Developmental Behavioural Modelling (DBM – a systemic approach using fractal modelling to create and apply models in all levels of human experience) and Francine Shapiro's Eye Movement Desensitization Reprocessing (EMDR – therapeutic handling of unprocessed blockages and traumas through guided eye movements – not strict NLP, but utilizing similar premises; Connirae and Steve Andreas developed a similar NLP process – Eye Movement Integrator – at about the same time).

This chapter has covered some of the better known NLP approaches and techniques. The next section of the book goes on to explore how some of the techniques we have been discussing can be applied in your everyday life.

SECTION TWO

This part of the book contains the practical elements of NLP; how you can use the techniques and approaches in your own life. The chapters present some of the detail with which NLP works and it is worth remembering that these detailed techniques and approaches together combine to produce a total framework for achievement enhancement.

The chapters which follow are divided into contextual areas. Chapter 4 covers personal growth, chapter 5 covers relationships and chapter 6 covers work and business. In order to give a shape to the applications chapters, certain techniques have been selected to illustrate how you can apply NLP in your own daily activities. All the techniques are useful in a wide range of situations, however, so when reading about, and practising, them, you can also transfer their use into contexts which are different from those illustrated.

4 · PERSONAL GROWTH

*We all change throughout life; this is an inevitable process. Without change we would stagnate and fail to keep up with the altering world around us. Growth, however, is another thing altogether. People have different definitions of growth, but as a working premise we can take the idea that growth involves reaching different **levels** of thinking, feeling, behaving or being. So growth is different from change in that it is **beyond** what currently exists, rather than simply different.*

If you think about the various areas of your life, you can consider to what extent you are achieving the levels of development, or success, you desire. It may be that, in some areas, you do not know what you would like to attain, or it may be that there are areas which are, at present, something of a blank book – you may not even know of their existence. Or it may be that you know what you would like to achieve, but do not know how to bring about the changes which are required.

In this chapter we will take some areas of personal growth and consider how NLP can help you attain a higher stage of development. We will also explore in more depth some of the techniques we covered in chapter 3 and apply them in the following areas:

- *self-esteem, resourcefulness and emotional control (what happens in your mind)*
- *health, fitness and sports performance (what happens in your body)*
- *learning and skills development (what happens in your performance)*
- *spirituality (what happens in your awareness)*

Processes

Before embarking on this exploration, there are two processes which are useful to consider: self-awareness and movement. Let us consider each of these briefly.

SELF-AWARENESS

In order to make the most of the techniques discussed (and, in a broader context, to make the most of opportunities life presents to you), it helps if you have a reasonable degree of self-awareness. Self-awareness usually entails a recognition of what you are able to do, what you actually do, how you do it and the results of having done it; this includes your behaviour, your thoughts, your feelings and your beliefs, values and assumptions (as outlined in chapter 1).

MOVEMENT

Movement includes the process of change and progress. It is impossible to stand still in life, but knowing where you want to get to and how to get there is not always easy. NLP has a process which helps with this concept of movement; it has three elements, as follows:

- **present state**; in other words the situation which currently exists in relation to an issue. For example, if you do not yet know how to rollerskate, your current state is one of LACK OF EXPERIENCE.
- **desired state**; in other words what you want to achieve in relation to this issue. So, keeping the rollerskating

example, the desired state might be one of COMPETENT PERFORMANCE.

- the transition from present state to desired state; ie the **steps to take**. Here, you might HAVE LESSONS IN ROLLERSKATING.

So the two processes which inform the whole of this chapter, and indeed the two further applications chapters which follow, are self-awareness and movement. By understanding yourself, knowing where you are currently, what you would like to achieve and how to get there you have the foundation for achieving success.

The remainder of this chapter covers some common situations where you might wish to make changes in your life and gives suggestions as to how they might be tackled, using NLP. Each example involves using the process outlined above; ie identifying PRESENT SITUATION, DESIRED SITUATION and STEPS TO TAKE – the 'steps to take' include an appropriate NLP technique. If the precise examples do not apply to you, simply transfer the techniques to comparable situations of your own. The categories covered are as outlined above, ie, self-esteem, resourcefulness and emotional control, health, fitness and sports performance, learning and skills development, and spirituality.

SELF-ESTEEM, RESOURCEFULNESS AND EMOTIONAL CONTROL

Most of us have times when we feel self-assured and resourceful and times when we feel disempowered. Often we put the latter occasions down to external forces, saying things like 'They made me feel really bad', 'It gave me a problem' or 'I was a victim of circumstances'. In practice, however, we can all be responsible for our own thoughts, feelings, responses and behaviour and, however difficult or restricting circumstances may be, we have facilities for overcoming obstacles and problems. Of course, doing this may not always be easy and we may not always know exactly how to tackle difficult situations, but if we adopt a positive and practical approach, many things can be improved.

So what can NLP offer in this area? The most useful NLP techniques here are to do with mental processing; in other words using your mind to make changes in your perception and in your creativity. Let us take some examples of situations and see how they might be assisted by NLP.

The following technique will help if you sometimes have a low opinion of yourself, consider that your opinions have little value and nobody would want to listen to them, or believe that other people generally know more than you do and are more competent than you. If you try hard to please friends and family but simply have the feeling that whatever you do is not good enough, and if you find it hard to think of yourself as a success, you can benefit from this process.

With low self-esteem, it may be difficult even to think of things being different; however you might, as a desired situation, wish you could have interesting and worthwhile things to say to people. You might like to believe that you are capable of doing things well; for example cooking a meal or organizing an event.

So what can you do to make a change? You can use 'internal dialogue' to improve the way you feel about yourself. Internal dialogue relates to the 'inner voices' many of us have in our heads, telling us things about what we are doing and how others are responding to us. Sometimes these inner voices may be our own voice, sometimes they may be voices of people we know; often they are negative and critical.

You may, at present, imagine yourself saying things like, 'I'm not very good at things', 'I can't do things right', 'What I think isn't important'. You may imagine other people saying negative things about you such as, 'He isn't very interesting', 'She didn't do that very well'. With such negative dialogue going on, low self esteem could easily follow.

To change the situation, you could change what you say to yourself; perhaps: 'I *am* capable at the things I do', 'I *can* find some interesting things to say to this person', 'I *am* as valuable as other people'. You could also let any imagined criticisms from other people become less audible in your head (imagining the voices becoming quieter or more distant) and substitute more positive thoughts; for example imagining people saying they have enjoyed talking to you and complimenting you on things you have done. To do this successfully, make the voices positive sounding, with a pleasant tone and loud enough to be convincing.

This goes beyond just positive thinking as it is important to *actually imagine hearing* the positive words in your head, as if they are really happening. Because your mind does not differentiate between fact and fiction (imagine a lemon slice in your mouth and notice if your mouth waters even though the lemon is not real), you can put new voices into your imagination and your mind will accept them as if they were real. In this way it is possible to have a new perception of reality and a new, more positive, self-concept.

RESOURCEFULNESS – CONFIDENCE

Resourcefulness is about being able to generate thoughts and feelings which are supportive to what you wish to achieve. The previous example was about making your thoughts more positive; the next example is about enhancing your feelings of confidence.

Suppose you have to give a speech at a wedding. If you have never liked speaking in public you might think you will sound dull, look ill at ease and feel anxious. You may not think you can project your voice well and may think you will be unable to remember what to say. Overall you may find it hard to have a perception of yourself as a natural, witty speaker.

What you might prefer would be to be able to stand up confidently, control your nerves, remember what to say, sound interesting and amusing and look as if you are enjoying making the speech. However, because you have been used to feeling awkward and ill at ease on past occasions, your body probably gets used to taking up the posture it remembers from previous uncomfortable experiences.

So what you can do to make a change is to re-access past feelings which are more positive. You may well have past experiences of feeling much more confident and at ease (not necessarily anything to do with making speeches). At such times you are able to move freely, breathe easily and look at people in a friendly and welcoming way. To feel better at the wedding, you can reaccess such feelings and, by doing so, recreate the posture, movement and gestures which accompany them.

So you could remember a specific time when you felt very confident. You can access this time by remembering what you could see (whether you were indoors or outdoors; what colours and shapes you could see, what scenery or furnishings); you could also remember what you could hear at the time (whether there were people talking, music playing or whether it was very quiet and peaceful); you could remember any physical sensations (whether you were warm or cool, standing or sitting, holding or touching anything) and you could remember if you had a taste in your mouth from eating or drinking or if there was a scent in the air. Finally you could remember the feeling of confidence and relaxation and notice where in your body this was (for example, your head, stomach, chest or all over).

Once you have gone through this process, you will have reminded yourself that you *can* feel confident, and what that is like physically. Once you have recalled this, your body will begin to take up a similar stance to the one it had on the past occasion; your posture and movement may shift, your breathing may alter, your expression may change. Now all you have to do is to capture this physiological change in your memory, by noting exactly what your posture, movement, breathing and expression is. When you have to make the speech, by adopting this posture, movement, breathing pattern and facial expression you will look and sound confident and will feel much more able to carry out the task in a competent and enjoyable manner.

RESOURCEFULNESS – PATIENCE

If you have a relative (let us assume it is your mother) who is elderly and has developed Alzheimer's disease, she may forget what she has said and keep repeating things, wander out of the house and have to be tracked down, put the kettle on a hotplate and boil it dry, and wake you up in the night by wandering around and knocking things over. You may be stressed by having to deal with this situation and find yourself getting frustrated, tired and snappy. The whole situation may weigh you down. You know your mother cannot help what she does and you would probably like to see a lighter side to the situation, rather than becoming angry.

What you can do is use the 'anchoring' technique to help yourself change your response. Anchoring simply means making an association between a situation and a trigger, so that when the trigger is activated, the response to the situation can be changed (*see* chapter 3). You probably already have many negative anchors (triggers) for your present situation. For example, your mother's voice may act as a trigger to make you feel irritated; the sight of the kettle she boils dry could be a trigger for you feeling anxious.

It would not be appropriate for you to disregard your feelings, but it probably *would* be better for you to have more resourceful feelings than irritation and anxiety. So what you could do is to think of a time when you were able to be really patient. Think yourself back into this situation just as in the previous example about public speaking. Once you really remember the past situation, you can give yourself a trigger (for example biting the end of your tongue very gently), so that this trigger is associated with the feeling of patience. A few practice runs will help you associate the trigger with the memory.

Now when you hear your mother's voice or see the kettle you can *bite your tongue*. This should generate a feeling of patience, leaving you to decide whether you actually need to do more about the situation or whether you can just allow it to wash over you in a calm way. Anchoring is a powerful technique, and one which can be really helpful in becoming more positive and resourceful.

EMOTIONAL CONTROL — HANDLING TRAUMATIC FEELINGS

Many people have had experiences which have made a major impact on them. Often these experiences are very positive and life-enhancing, but sometimes they result in overwhelming feelings such as anger, grief, resentment and fear. Sometimes these feelings persist, or resurface over a period of time.

The NLP approach to trauma is generally forward- rather than backward-looking. In other words it does not work by getting the person to relive the past experience in order to exorcise it, nor does it work by exploring the reasons for a memory persisting (ie an analytical approach based on the content of the memory). NLP usually works through helping the person elicit their 'desired state' – what they would like instead – and then finding ways of assisting them to access that alternative way of being.

So some 'desired states' might be acceptance rather than anger, appreciation rather than grief, tolerance instead of resentment and calmness rather than fear. To achieve these states, a technique which is often used by therapists involves you in 'viewing' the traumatic event in a detached way, so that it is possible to experience the event as an 'observer' rather than relive it as a participant. By detaching yourself in this way, the feelings associated with the event become distanced and it is possible to review what has happened, and respond to it in a more appropriate manner.

If you wish to work on a personal issue of this nature, an NLP psychotherapist will be able to help you (*see* Useful Addresses for details of how to find a therapist).

HEALTH AND FITNESS

People nowadays are much more aware of the benefits which come from good health and a high degree of personal fitness. While not everyone wishes to be a top sportsperson, there are many elements of physical health and fitness which can be achieved by the average person.

WEIGHT CONTROL

Many people are somewhat overweight, lack energy and feel their health is being affected because their weight prevents them being as active as they would like. If you would like to lose weight (without becoming waif-like), you should find the following exercise useful.

When you look in a mirror you see your present self looking back out and your mind has only this image to work with. Although you may want to change how you look, you may find it hard to picture yourself any differently and it is important to believe that your desired state is achievable if you are to make progress.

It seems that our minds are best motivated when they have a real goal to work towards and it helps when this goal is represented in a visual way, so what you can do is express your goal as if you had already achieved it, and then picture it as if it were real. So, you might say: 'I exercise regularly; I weigh . . . stone and I can get into size . . . clothes'. You could then make a mental image of the new you. This image should be as motivating as possible, which means it will probably be bright, colourful, close up, with movement and activity.

Once your mind has seen this picture, and keeps on seeing it, you are likely to be more motivated to achieve your result (you really are 'keeping it in mind'). NLP suggests that everyone has their own optimum way of visualizing particular things; for example seeing them at a certain distance, a certain angle, a certain size and so forth. You may need a little help to identify your own most successful visualization process so that you can really make progress towards your goal. You will still have to do the work of eating sensibly and exercising appropriately if you are to lose weight, but the mental image will keep you focused and motivated to do this. (And if you are not good at visualizing, you can substitute a different mental process; for example using 'internal dialogue' to help you achieve results, although you may prefer to develop your visualization skills through further reading and practice (*see* Section three).

MOTIVATION TO EXERCISE

Do you find it hard to keep motivated to exercise, perhaps getting bored working out at the gym, especially while using equipment which takes up quite a bit of time? The unchanging surroundings in these places often fails to provide stimulation to the senses, which can make time seem to pass slowly and result in demotivation.

If you imagine being somewhere else, your mind can become absorbed in this experience and it can seem as if time passes faster. As an example, you could think of a real place, which you enjoy visiting. This may be a distant location or may be close to home; perhaps even something as simple as the local shops.

Now, what you can do is imagine, while you are on the jogger or other equipment, that you are taking a walk (or run) to the shops. Imagine doing this in real time, so that you feel your feet stepping on the ground, see the sights you would actually pass on the real walk, hear any sounds which would be there, feel the temperature, smell any scents in the air and so on.

As you go on your imaginary walk, your mind should become more stimulated, your conscious awareness of your present surroundings should diminish and your thoughts can become more self-absorbed and imaginative. In much less time than usual you will have competed your exercise and also had the mental stimulation of the imaginary walk, Next time you can choose a different walk or even a different context, such as an imaginary discussion with a friend, working on a problem which needs to be solved or planning a future event. All these processes, when made real enough, will act to distort time and make the activity seem faster.

You will still need to pay conscious attention to your exercise technique, but with practice you can do this, as well as allowing your mind to relax when it is not needed for conscious activity.

SPORTS PERFORMANCE

Much has been written about enhancing sports performance through mental as well as physical processes, and there are books on specific sports as well as general guides to improvement. In this section we will deal with just one element – the use of mental practice to enhance skills.

It has been found that mental practice is extremely effective in developing skills. With real life practice, some moves will be excellent and some will be less good. With mental practice, however, it is possible to repeat, in your mind, time after time, a move which you remember doing in the past. If the original move was really good, the imaginary ones you repeat in your mind will be just as good. It seems that this repeated imagined activity somehow generates nerve connections in the mind, which set up pathways for repeated excellence – and, because there will be no errors in your mind, the repeated movements will enhance the skill when put into practice in real life.

As an example of this, if you take the sport of fencing and wish to be able to improve a particular move, you can imagine in your mind the various elements of that move as you have done it in the past. For example, some of the things you can imagine include the weight and shape of the sword's handle in your hand, the direction and speed of your arm as you execute the move, the sound of the blade as it meets that of your opponent, the rhythm and pace of the movement as it takes place. By reliving this experience, you can mentally rehearse the move, adding in any aspects which will refine and improve it. When you come to do the move for real, the mental practice will have helped your development of the skill.

ALLEVIATING ALLERGIES

Many people are basically fit and healthy but, from time to time, find they have medical complaints which are slow to clear. Using NLP techniques, sometimes in conjunction with hypnosis, can often provide ways of alleviating symptoms and combatting causes of illness, although it is important to emphasize that NLP, or other non-medical techniques, should not be used as a substitute for professional medical help where this is the most appropriate approach to a condition.

Let us take allergies as an example. If you have had an allergic reaction to something, it may well have been diagnosed medically and treated with drugs. If this has worked, you may be satisfied with the result. If, however, drugs have not produced the effect you need, or if you wish to explore other means of alleviation, you may be interested in a technique which appears to work well for some people (Dilts, Smith and Hallbom, *Belief*, Metamorphosis Press, 1990).

This technique is based on the concept that an allergy is simply a mistake which has been made by the immune system, whereby something which is basically harmless causes the body to respond in an inappropriate way. The technique, through which you would need to be guided by a trained practitioner, involves finding something which is comparable to the thing which triggers the allergic response, but to which you have no allergic response. You would then be helped to imagine yourself with this non-threatening thing, build up a positive response to it and then transfer that positive response to the original thing to which your body reacted by producing the allergic response.

The NLP approach to allergies is just one example of how people can be helped to respond in different ways to medical conditions, both physical and mental. Some other areas in which good results have been claimed for NLP include arthritis, poor eyesight, tinnitus, pain control (including terminal illnesses), anxiety, depression, phobias and eating disorders.

With medical conditions, in addition to the techniques described already, the NLP approaches used may include the following:

- reframing (experiencing a condition from a different perspective; such as considering a broken leg as an opportunity to catch up on reading); sometimes there are hidden benefits in illnesses which a different way of thinking can reveal, and sometimes viewing an illness in a new light can help alleviate symptoms

- sub-modality work (making changes in how your mind represents the situation; for example picturing yourself as fit and healthy, or hearing your voice saying you are improving on a daily basis)
- programming for control (for example imagining pain levels as points on a dial and then making it possible to mentally shift the dial position in order to lessen the pain experienced)
- shifting beliefs (for example believing you are capable of seeing without glasses)
- using hypnotic trance states (for example speeding up the healing process after an operation through suggestion techniques – a process which is increasingly being used in conventional surgery)
- visualization (for example imagining cancer cells as snowballs being melted by the heat of the body's immune system)
- parts work (identifying 'parts' of a person which are responsible for creating symptoms and then identifying more creative parts which can produce more desirable results)
- analysis of behaviour patterns (analysing what a person does and substituting other activities which are likely to produce greater benefits)

If you are interested in finding out more about such approaches to medical conditions, NLP therapists will be able to help you (*see* Useful Addresses for how to contact a therapist).

LEARNING AND SKILLS DEVELOPMENT

We all learn and develop as we go through life, sometimes deliberately, at other times in an unplanned way. Learning encompasses knowledge, understanding and skills development, and all of these help us enhance our performance of the various activities in which we are engaged.

SPELLING

Perhaps you think you are a poor speller. Some people have problems with spelling because they have dyslexia but even if you do not have dyslexia you may just find it difficult to remember how words are composed.

If you would like to be able to spell words easily, especially in situations such as making a job application when you want what you write to reflect well on you, the NLP strategy for spelling should help. This strategy was developed largely by Robert Dilts, with other members of the original group at Santa Cruz (*see* chapter 2) also being involved, and in fact it was this work on the spelling strategy which started off the broader work on strategies which has become a major foundation of NLP.

Research indicates that people who are good spellers have one particular thing in common: they are good at picturing things and visualize the word they wish to spell as they think about it. If you wish to spell better, it can help to embark on a programme of developing your visual sense. When you come across a word you need to spell, you can look at it in print, then, maintaining a positive feeling, close your eyes and picture it on the page. It will almost certainly help if you move your eyes upwards as you do this, as this seems to help to activate the part of the brain which produces images. As you practise this skill, you should find it easier to 'see' the word and when this happens you will find you can spell it both backwards and forwards, if you choose. If you would like to know more about the spelling strategy, of which only part has been described here, it has been popularized in *Meta-cation* by Sid Jacobson.

STUDYING, LEARNING AND TAKING EXAMINATIONS

If you (or your child) find it hard to concentrate at school or college and if sometimes, although you try to pay attention to a teacher or lecturer, you do not seem to be able to focus on what is being said, and wonder how you will get through the course, this next technique may be useful.

If you want to find your lessons interesting and remember what you are told, so that you can enjoy taking any examinations and showing what you can do, you can begin by identifying how you learn best. People all have individual ways of learning; these may include picturing things, hearing things, using logic, using numbers, doing physical movements, working with others, working alone and so forth. In particular, NLP and Accelerated Learning have shown how the use of all five senses (sight, sound, touch, taste and smell) can enhance a learning process. If you find it hard to learn simply by listening, it may be because you are not very auditory (not good at using your sense of hearing and manipulation of words).

If your teacher/lecturer does not know much about Accelerated Learning, he may rely heavily on *telling* students things, *reading to them*, and getting them to *read books*. This approach does not work well for people who are very visual or for those who need to get a real grasp of their subjects. If this applies to you, it may be that you learn much better when you are *shown* things or when you can *get a feel* for what they are and how they work.

So you could take a number of steps to help yourself learn. First you can draw yourself 'mind maps' (a concept developed by Tony Buzan and illustrated in books such as *The Mind Map Book*) to give yourself a good picture of each topic and how its different elements interrelate. A mind map is a diagram, using words, pictures, colours and interconnecting lines, to put a topic together as a visual image, as the illustration overleaf shows.

There is good evidence that effective students naturally use the mind mapping process, even if they have not been shown it by someone else; work by Cricket Kemp has recently explored this with pupils in colleges in England. Using this technique will help you see things for yourself, rather than just hearing them said by a teacher.

If visual approaches do not work either, it may be that a more 'hands on' approach will work for you. To do this, you can work out a way of making things more tangible; for example if you are studying movement in a biology class, you

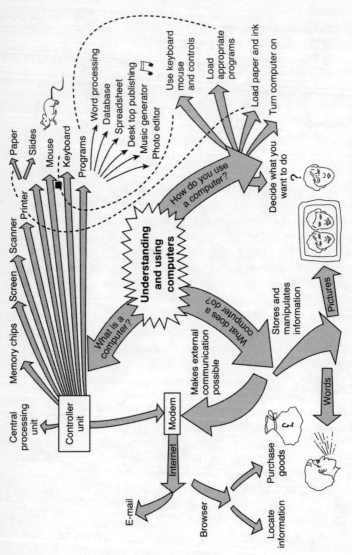

A mind map about understanding and using computers

could feel your own joints to get a sense of how movement occurs; this may be more helpful to you than simply seeing diagrams of joints in books.

There are many books on Accelerated Learning techniques; *see* the Bibliography for examples.

AWARENESS OF HIGHER LEVELS

Personal growth is not only about developments in knowledge and skills, it is also about the relationship between tangible, existential elements of life and those elements which cannot be quantified and physically handled, but bring an awareness of forces beyond our conscious existence. Do note that, in NLP, spirituality is not about religion or religious belief (although it could be for any particular individual).

There are ways of using NLP in order to access personal understanding and development of spiritual awareness. The following examples use modelling (*see* chapter 3) as a process for expanding awareness.

If you have a partner who attends religious services each week and, although you have no inclination towards organized religion, you feel a little left out at times, or if you would like to find out how people bring wider experiences into their everyday life, you should find this next section of interest.

To explore these possibilities, you can adopt the NLP process of modelling (copying) people who have some belief in 'what is beyond'. To do this you could:

- read about the different kinds of belief people have
- research what people do in order to extend their spiritual awareness – meditation, observation of patterns in nature, and so forth
- do exercises designed to bring about shifts in perception, for example imagining taking on the perspective of a higher being, or your own 'higher self', by imagining how

such a 'higher entity' might perceive people and how they go about their lives (exercises designed by Penny Tompkins and James Lawley)

- find your 'core values' by identifying things you really want and then what you would gain if you had them (see *Core Transformation* by Connirae Andreas, Real People Press, 1979, for more on this topic)
- find a symbol or metaphor for your purpose, sense of direction or mission in life, or for a connection with something greater than yourself (for example thinking of your purpose as if it were a beacon shining brightly; thinking of your sense of direction as an upward spiral or thinking of your connection with an entity beyond yourself as a magnetic field)

SENSE OF PURPOSE

If you sometimes feel you lack a sense of purpose in your life and find yourself very occupied with day-to-day affairs, while being uncertain of where they are leading, or if you would like to know what it is that you contribute and whether it is part of any greater whole beyond yourself, you may find this exercise (based on David Gordon's Meaningful Existence model) helpful.

Think of a number of times when you are really 'being yourself'; times when you feel fulfilled and happy. You can write down the details, or get a friend to listen to you talking; then you can find a few key words, phrases or events which seem to keep cropping up in the events. For example, you might find that these times are about helping others, bringing about change and having fun. You can then, with your friend's help if necessary, find a phrase which sums up your personal mission via these words; for example: 'I help people create things they want in a light hearted way.' By using your own experience as a basis for finding a common thread, you can become more aware of a personal mission which can go beyond your normal everyday existence. Making such connections is one way to gaining some spiritual awareness.

These last exercises have all focused on modelling, either other people or yourself, in order to develop. Role modelling is the process which really started NLP; the attempt to observe, quantify and transfer to others the elements of effective performance.

In any area where you would like to improve or develop, it is well worth finding yourself a role model to emulate. Role modelling, by the way, does not mean 'becoming' the same person as the role model; it simply means utilizing a part of his or her behaviour in a way which is appropriate for you. This is how we all learn; from our earliest days we copy those around us in order to try out, and use, different behaviours. NLP just suggests we continue this into adult life and make a practice of learning from others.

There is one particular NLP technique which uses this role modelling process in a very simple way; it is called the New Behaviour Generator and was developed by Judith DeLozier. This process allows you to try out new behaviours in your mind before using them in real life, which gives you an opportunity to review the behaviour and check whether it would, in fact, be appropriate behaviour for you to copy.

The process involves visualizing and so you may wish to practise the following basic visualization techniques before beginning:

- Look at an illustration in a book; describe to yourself (out loud or in your head) whatever you can see; close your eyes and remember as much of the illustration as you can, including the colours, the shapes, the proximity of one part of the illustration to another, and so on.
- Look at yourself in a mirror; again, say what you see in as much detail as possible; close your eyes and recall that detail (the colour of your eyes, the shape of your mouth, the length of your hair, and so on).
- Think about a place you visited some time ago; keep your eyes open and remember as much as you can about how the place looked (scenery, buildings, decorations, colours, shapes and so on); close your eyes and notice if it is easier to remember those same elements.

89

- Close your eyes and imagine picturing the following: a bicycle, an apple, a teapot, an elephant, a beach, clouds in the sky.
- Close your eyes and imagine picturing the following: a giant ant; a tiny aeroplane; a soft table; a hard blade of grass; a green pigeon; a blue banana; a camera with hands; a transparent person.

Now you have done these exercises, have a go at the New Behaviour Generator:

1 Find a quiet place and sit or lie in a comfortable position.
2 Think of something you would like to be able to do, or something you already do which you would like to do better.
3 Think of a person (your role model) whom you have observed doing that thing; this may be a person you know yourself, or it may be someone you have seen on television.
4 In your mind, make an image of the person doing that behaviour and watch it as clearly as you can. See how the person sits, stands or moves; watch his gestures and the expression on his face; imagine the sound of his voice; notice how other people are reacting to him. Once you have done this, check that you would like to be able to do this yourself.
5 In your mind, substitute yourself for the other person and, as if you were distanced from yourself, watch yourself behaving in the same way. Remember, this is not about being the other person; simply copying one element of his behaviour. Again, check that you would still like to do things in that way.
6 Now imagine 'stepping into' your mental image and feeling what it would be like to behave in that way. Notice how your body feels when you behave like that; notice the sound of your voice if you are speaking; notice how any other people around seem to respond to you. Really become aware of what it is like to behave like that now. Again, check that that behaviour is consistent with who you are.

7 Think of a situation in the near future when it would be desirable and appropriate to use that behaviour. In your mind, make a mental image of behaving in that way. If you are happy with that, move on to the next step.
8 Again, imagine stepping into that experience and really feel what it is like to behave like that in the real situation. Enjoy the experience of your new skill.

Doing this exercise gives your mind the sense that you have already behaved like that in reality; when you come to do it for real, it will be easier and more enjoyable.

Last Points

This chapter of the book has presented some of the techniques and approaches which distinguish NLP's contribution to the development of personal excellence. The approaches and techniques discussed can be used to encourage imagination and problem solving at both conscious and unconscious levels and can contribute to both personal development and healing.

NLP takes a holistic view of change work, so that shifts in one element, such as behaviour, thoughts, feelings or beliefs, impinge on others in a systemic way. This means that whenever a change process is undertaken, its impact on the individual as a whole needs to be taken into account.

Scientific research is proving the links between mind and body which have until recently been the subject of debate; with evidence accumulating on the importance of positive mental and emotional states on physical health and personal achievement, NLP has much to offer in the field of personal enhancement.

5 · SOCIAL RELATIONSHIPS

Having considered personal growth, we can now move on to ways of enhancing interactions with others and this chapter will give you a range of ways to create and maintain good relationships.

There are many occasions when we need to come into contact with other people in our personal life. Some of these include social events with friends or colleagues, family events, dealings with neighbours, using professional services (doctors, accountants, teachers, electricians and so forth). The list is lengthy and varied.

Each of the groups mentioned above has its own characteristics, but there are common threads running through them all. In each case, the interaction is enhanced if an effective relationship can be created quickly and maintained as long as required. NLP offers ways of doing just this – developing good and lasting relationships with other people.

Personal communications plays a major part in dealing with other people and there are a range of ways in which you can communicate. Communications involve both what you say (the content of a communication) and the way in which you say it (the process of a communication). You can also communicate verbally (through words: orally if spoken, non-orally if written) or non-verbally (through ways which do not involve spoken or written language – eg appearance, gesture, voice tone and so forth).

Interactions may be on a one-to-one basis or with several people; they may be face to face or on the telephone; they may be through the internet or they may be via written communications, such as letters or faxes. On the whole, the term 'social relationships' implies face-to-face contact, but establishing relationships in some of the other ways listed above is also important and requires equivalent skills.

If you have ever felt at a loss as to how to deal with others, if you have felt anxious about meeting people or making small talk, if you have been concerned about dealing with those in authority, if you have worried about doing something embarrassing when in company, if you have found it difficult to assert yourself, if you have wondered how to handle conflict with or between others, or if you have found it difficult to control your feelings or express yourself fluently, then this section can help you.

There are a number of steps involved in dealing with others; these include having an objective, planning what to do or say, managing how you feel, using observation and listening skills, communicating effectively, gaining rapport and influencing. It is also vital to be flexible and to monitor and review what you do, so that you can assess how effective it has been and whether to do something similar again in the future. We will be covering some of these topics in chapter 6, on work and business applications, so will concentrate here on the steps which are more to do with person-to-person contact. These steps are:

- using observation skills
- shifting perspective
- creating and maintaining rapport
- using language flexibly
- being persuasive and influential

USING OBSERVATION SKILLS

Noticing how other people are behaving and reacting is a very useful skill. It is surprising how often people 'mind read' others' behaviour and say things like 'She looked very bored', 'He was clearly confused', or 'They sounded rather aloof'. All these observations could have been correct, but equally could have been a misinterpretation of someone else's behaviour. For example, yawning *could* indicate boredom, but could just as easily indicate tiredness or lack of oxygen.

To ensure that you understand another person, it is useful to treat their behaviour simply as information, without evaluating it; and then to check what the person is really feeling or thinking. It is possible to do this directly by asking about that person's thoughts or feelings and it is also possible to check by testing out your own observations and looking for other evidence to support your interpretation.

The NLP term for observation is 'sensory acuity' – using your senses to pick up signals. If you would like to become more skilled at observation, have a go at the following activities.

- Watch people on public transport. Notice how they look just before they reach the stop where they get off. Begin to notice how their behaviour changes at this stage – for example, where they look, whether they shift position, when they reach for any things they have put on the floor. Watching in this way will help you become aware of the early signs of reactions to circumstances.
- Ask a person you know if she will help with an exercise. Ask her to sit in a chair and then think of a person she likes. As she thinks of this person, notice her posture in the chair, any movement she is making with her hands or feet, her head position, her eye movements, whether her mouth changes (eg widens or turns up), where her eyes are focusing (in the distance or close up) and the direction in which she is looking, etc. Then ask her to think of a person she does not like and notice the same elements, this time looking for differences between her appearance when thinking about the first person and when thinking about the second

person. Finally, ask her to think of either the first or the second person (the person she likes or the person she dislikes) and try to guess which of the two it is. Repeat the process until you are correct each time and then have a go at doing it with someone else.

- Watch and listen to a person you are with frequently. Become aware of exactly how she looks and sounds when in different states; for example, what tone of voice goes with pleasure or irritation; what posture goes with energy or lethargy; what eye movements go with past memories or future expectations.

Doing these exercises will help you hone your observation skills and become more sensitive and responsive to other people's experiences. By enhancing your understanding of, and responsiveness towards, others, you are likely to find that your relationships with them improve and misunderstandings become easier to avoid.

SHIFTING PERSPECTIVE

The NLP term for shifting perspectives is 'taking on different perceptual positions'. People often use phrases which refer to positions, such as saying: 'If I were in your position I would do things differently.' This kind of statement recognizes the fact that people do differ in how they act and that we can imagine being in someone else's 'position'.

NLP refers to a whole series of perceptual positions and these have been illustrated in chapter 3. The point of considering these positions is to enable people to understand how others view and react to, situations. You might like to have a go at using different perspectives in the following situations.

- **Shopping**. If you have to stand in a queue, imagine that you are in the position of the shop assistant (ie take on what is called 'second position'); this will give you an idea of what is going on for that person. Then imagine what it is like for the person behind you in the queue (a further 'second position' shift). Then imagine how the entire queue looks to other people wandering around the shop (ie

95

taking on 3rd, or 'Meta-position'). Each time you shift perspective in this way it gives you an insight into other people's situations and responses.

- **Family occasions**. If you bring a new visitor to meet members of your family, imagine taking on the perspectives of other individual members of your family ('second position') and think how your friend might appear to them; then consider how your family might come across to your friend (adopting 'second position' in relation to your friend); then, finally, imagine how you, together with your family, come across to your friend (taking 'Meta-position' in relation to yourself and the family).

These differing perspectives can help you tune into other people's experience and see things in a new light. When you take on other people's perspectives, they are more likely to feel you understand them and be more responsive to your dealings with them.

CREATING AND MAINTAINING RAPPORT

When people are getting on well together we say they are 'in rapport'. You will probably be aware that there are some people with whom you feel really at ease and others to whom you find it harder to relate. Sometimes you can meet someone for the first time and immediately feel comfortable with him, as if you had known him for years. What is it that makes the difference?

NLP offers a simple way of thinking about rapport. The principle is that people tend to get on well with others who are similar to them in some way, for example, people who share similar interests, live in similar houses, like similar food or music, wear similar clothes or think in similar ways. The idea behind this is that if you look in a mirror you see something familiar and, if you look at another person and see something similar, it is familiar and not threatening, therefore making yourself similar in some ways tends to make you more acceptable.

NLP can help you create and maintain rapport with others. The underlying principle is that, if you do not have automatic rapport with someone, you can create it by making yourself like that person in some way or fitting in with what she does; for example, by being quiet if the other person is trying to study, or by talking about an activity you know the other person likes.

If you are trying to be like another person, there are different ways in which you can do this. The first is to mimic her. Mimicking is often very badly received, however, as it can result in the person feeling ridiculed and embarrassed. The second way in which you can make yourself like another person is to mirror her. This means doing exactly as she does. Mirroring can be very obvious and overdone, however. A better process is what NLP calls 'Matching'. Matching means doing things in a similar way to the other person, but doing the *minimum* necessary to make yourself like them, not the maximum.

Matching is a natural process; when people are getting on well together they naturally do things in a synchronized way – just look at couples walking along the street together and notice that they are generally taking steps at the same time as each other. If you match other people, they are more likely to feel at ease with you.

Matching is a versatile and influential tool, and well worth practising. For example, suppose you are in a railway train, in a corner seat near a window, and sitting opposite you, also in a corner seat, is another person. He is leaning to one side, with his legs crossed, tapping one toe up and down constantly, occasionally glancing out of the window. To match the person you might simply adopt a similarly relaxed posture; not necessarily identical, but relaxed rather than stiff. Or each time the other person looked out of the window, you might do so (a few seconds later in order to make it less obvious); or, instead of looking out of the window, you might glance along the carriage. These are all ways of being similar without copying exactly. Have a go at this yourself the next time you are travelling.

We have talked about matching posture, movement and gestures, but there are many other things which could be matched, such as thought processes. If you are with someone who always thinks long term, you could talk to them about long-term issues rather than short-term ones. If you are with someone who is clearly making mental images of plants for her garden you could talk in graphic terms about other plants so that she could see these too in her 'mind's eye'. What you are doing in these instances is considering how the other person is thinking (either in relation to the concepts she is using, or in relation to how her mind is creating her thoughts) and then matching her inner processes of thinking.

You can also match people's emotional state; if you are with someone who is depressed or upset, he will probably feel better if you talk quietly and do not overwhelm him with fast movements and gestures; if you are with someone who is excited, he will probably respond better if you also demonstrate excitement rather than detachment.

An important element of matching is to maintain what NLP refers to as 'congruence', ie consistency in what you do. If, for example, you were asked what you thought of an event and you said you thought it went well, while at the same time shaking your head, the other person would receive a mixed message. Congruence is about selecting your actions, or responses, and then making sure they are consistent with each other.

Finally, there may be times when matching would not be helpful; for example if someone is taking up too much of your time and you want them to leave you in peace, when a discussion has reached a stalemate and there needs to be a change in energy, or when you are being harassed and wish to bring the interaction to a fast end. In such cases, 'mismatching', ie doing the opposite of what the other person is doing, is probably a better process to engage in.

USING LANGUAGE FLEXIBLY

A major feature of relating to others is the way in which language is used to communicate. Each language has its own unique characteristics, and each individual person has a unique way of using words. Because of this diversity in communications, it is essential to be able to exercise flexibility in how one uses words so that communications can be geared very specifically to the person or people concerned.

NLP has much to offer the serious communicator. We have already considered some of the non-verbal elements involved in relating to others; this section will give you some ways of using words more effectively in your interactions with different people.

NLP has two basic language models, as we discussed in chapter 2. The first is called the Meta-Model, and originated from the work of Bandler and Grinder. The second is called the Milton Model and is based on the way in which Milton Erickson, a famous psychiatrist and hypnotherapist, conducted his interactions with his clients. As with the Meta-Model, these patterns were isolated and described by Bandler and Grinder as they studied the way in which Dr Erickson worked.

The Meta-Model gives ways of being precise with language, in order to achieve clarity of communication and understanding; the Milton Model relies heavily on suggestion, indirect language, metaphor and implied directions. Both are enormously useful in both day-to-day interactions and professional activities.

If you want to deal with others more effectively, it can help to use both the Meta-Model and the Milton Model appropriately, to improve your communication skills. Let us take some day-to-day occurrences and see how the use of one or other model can help or hinder.

Suppose your car has developed a fault and you wish to have it sorted out by your local garage. Here are two possible conversations you might have:

Car mechanic: What's the problem?
You: The car's making some kind of noise, from time to time; it seems to be coming from the back.

Car mechanic: What's the problem?
You: There's a loud grating noise, which is coming from the

near side, towards the back. I can hear it when I put the brakes on, but only when the car is very warm.

The first description is Milton Model language: non-specific. Listen to some of the words: SOME KIND OF noise. From TIME TO TIME. From THE BACK. The second description is Meta-Model language: much more precise. These words include: LOUD, GRATING, NEAR SIDE, WHEN I PUT THE BRAKES ON, ONLY when the car is very WARM.

In such a situation where precise information is required, Meta-Model language is most useful, making things clearer for the other person.

Now contrast this example with a different situation. A teacher is giving a class some homework to do.

Teacher: I'd like you to write an essay about your last holiday. Say where you went, what you did and who you met.

Teacher: I'd like you to produce something on a recent holiday. There are lots of interesting things about holidays: places, people, activities and so on. You can think about what you would like to include, such as your feelings about the holiday, things you learned, and so on.

In these examples, the first teacher made the task very prescriptive, saying things such as 'write' and 'say where you went' (using precise 'Meta-Model' type language). The second teacher left a lot to the individual pupil's imagination, saying things like 'produce something', 'interesting things', 'what you would like to include'; using this Milton Model language, it is possible to encourage people to think for themselves, be creative and innovative and consider their own personal approach to tasks. Using Meta-Model language is likely to limit this kind of activity and produce a narrower response.

BEING PERSUASIVE AND INFLUENTIAL

The final topic we will cover in this chapter is persuasion and influence and, long before NLP had a name, there were world famous writers producing books on how to 'win friends and influence people'. Now self-help and influencing skills are extremely common topics in NLP books and many of the most notable current writers and speakers on NLP concentrate on telling people how to promote themselves and their services or products through persuasion and influence. It is worth adding here that, when persuasion and influence are mentioned, people sometimes feel that what is really being discussed is manipulation. As already outlined in chapter 1, NLP is neutral as an approach; of course manipulation is possible in any situation, but if the approach of the person initiating the action is ethical, then this is unlikely to occur. And, as also mentioned previously, NLP practitioners generally do have respect for those with whom they come into contact instilled at an early stage in their training.

Many of the skills which underlie influence have already been covered in this chapter: using observation, shifting perspective, creating rapport and using language effectively. All these elements need to be in place before attempting to influence; if you do not use your observation, consider the other person's situation and create an effective relationship, it is unlikely that you will be able to influence significantly. Once you have established these foundations, however, you can take things one stage further.

So what are the additional elements which are involved in influencing? We will consider six points here:

- using the other person's motivational patterns to establish credibility and stimulate enthusiasm
- reinforcing verbal messages non-verbally
- using metaphor to create understanding
- moving conversations into the future
- using the person's preferred ways of perceiving to enhance your message
- providing evidence to meet the other person's requirements

USING MOTIVATIONAL PATTERNS

To hold someone's interest, it helps to know what motivates her. One way of finding this out is through her language patterns. Psychometric tests work on the principle that it is possible, through questioning, to elicit people's underlying personality and motivational traits, but it is possible to get similar information just through normal conversation. In NLP, these traits are referred to as 'meta-programmes' and there are several common ones which can easily be elicited.

Let us take just one of the motivational patterns which can be evoked. This pattern is to do with people's strength of belief in their own views, opinions and ways of doing things. A person who has strong views and defends them passionately can be termed 'internal'. The opposite of 'internal' is 'external', the term used to refer to a person who frequently needs feedback and endorsement from others.

To find out whether a person is internal or external you can ask some simple questions, but do remember that these traits are related to circumstances and can change over time, so that someone can be internal at work and external in relationships, or external when very young but more internal as time passes. A good question to ask is, 'How do you know you have done a good job at work?' or 'How do you know you have decorated a room well?' An internal person will say something like 'I just know I've done a good job' or 'I can see the results I have achieved', whereas an external person will say 'My boss tells me' or 'People say how nice it looks'. Once you know a person's motivational pattern you can use your matching skills to match their pattern in order to influence them. So to influence an internal person you might say '*You will know* how important it is to be on time', and to influence an external person you might say '*I would really like* you to be there on time'.

For more information on this kind of influencing process, do read Shelle Rose Charvet's excellent book, *Words That Change Minds* (*see* Bibliography) and also look at the LAB (Language and Behaviour) Profile, a questionnaire designed by Rodger Bailey to elicit a number of meta-programmes.

REINFORCING VERBAL MESSAGES NON-VERBALLY

NLP has a phrase for non-verbal support to messages; it is 'analogue marking'. Analogue markings are gestures (or could also be tone of voice and vocal emphasis). Reinforcing verbal messages can lend weight to your arguments. One way of doing this is by using hand gestures to demonstrate what you mean – for example moving your hands apart to show that something is a big issue.

It's a **BIG** issue

Another is vocally emphasizing part of a sentence (by saying the words louder or emphasizing them in some other way) to indicate its importance; for example, 'Please keep off the grass.'

USING METAPHOR TO ENHANCE UNDERSTANDING

Our unconscious minds frequently work with metaphor; this can be noted, for example, in dreams, where everyday and familiar people, places and events can take on distorted forms. Language is incredibly full of metaphor (and that phrase itself is a metaphor, of course, as language cannot actually be full of anything as it is not a container).

By using metaphor, you can influence people at many levels and it really helps to *match* their own metaphors where possible. So if someone says that looking after her disabled aunt is an *uphill struggle* you can respond, 'And when you are going uphill, it can be wonderful to find places to *rest and enjoy the view*, before continuing.' You have taken their language and used it to reply; your reply may then influence them to consider having a break.

MOVING CONVERSATIONS INTO THE FUTURE

This is an interesting concept. People often find it hard to make decisions or take action because they are stuck in the past, or immersed in the present. Giving them a sense of the future can be an incentive to move on. This can be done simply by using future tenses, an approach which comes from the NLP language models, in particular the Milton Model which utilizes indirect language patterns (*see* chapter 3). So, for example, you can say things like: '*When* you use this . . .', '*Once* you have done that . . .', and so on. Giving people an experience of the future can be a powerful influence.

USING PREFERRED WAYS OF PERCEIVING

We have spoken about the different senses people use (sight, sound, touch, taste, smell). Many people use all senses to a high degree, but some seem to place more weight on one or other of the senses. Some people are highly visual – designers maybe – while others are very kinaesthetic – perhaps dancers – and some very auditory – possibly musicians – and you can use these sensory 'preferences' as yet another means of matching a person to gain rapport. If you wish to influence someone in a new direction, it may be that you need to help him develop the use of senses which have been somewhat dormant.

For example, if you want to help someone furnish a room comfortably, but he is very auditory and does not have a highly developed kinaesthetic sense, you could start by *matching* their auditory preference by discussing how the room would sound with different furniture and then *lead* them into a more tactile awareness. So, you might say: 'Just imagine how it would sound with polished floorboards; your shoes would make a really loud noise as you walked (*auditory*); with soft carpet, however, it would muffle the sound (*auditory*). Just imagine how that soft carpet would feel (*kinaesthetic*) and how good it would feel (*kinaesthetic*) to just let your feet sink into that softness (*kinaesthetic*).' What you have done is to move the person into feelings from sounds – influencing him to have a new kind of experience.

PROVIDING EVIDENCE TO MEET SOMEONE'S REQUIREMENTS

Finally, if you wish to influence, it helps to show that there will be some benefit to the person concerned and that she has a way of knowing that what you are doing will be beneficial.

One way of doing this is by taking into account what NLP calls Evidence of Fulfilment (sometimes known as 'Complex Equivalence'). What this is about is the fact that when people have a belief, they also have things which, for them, are evidence of the existence of that belief. So if you wish to influence other people, it helps to have an insight into what informs their responses.

As an example of such evidence, suppose you would like to go out for a meal with a friend, but the response you get is: 'It's too much effort just now.' To find out what this means to the person (her evidence) you could say: 'How is it too much effort just now?'. She might reply: 'It means changing clothes and driving the car.' You might then say: 'Well, we could go somewhere informal where you don't need to dress up, and I will drive the car.' This works with the person's own beliefs about the situation and shows her that her needs can be met.

So this section has given you some ideas about persuasion and influence; NLP has much to offer in this area, helping you relate well to friends, acquaintances, partners, family, service providers and others. And creating and maintaining good social relationships can have effects on other areas of your life. It may make you feel more confident and self-assured; it may alleviate stress caused by conflict and disagreement; it may bring you more opportunities through extending the circle of people with whom you build contacts and interact. It is very well worth exploring further, but do remember to take the other person's wishes and needs into account, as well as your own, when you are using influencing skills – achieving 'win-win' situations benefits both parties.

6 · WORK AND BUSINESS

The last two chapters have been about ways of enhancing personal performance; this chapter moves into the world of work and considers how NLP can enhance work performance and relationships. Although NLP began life through the study of therapists, it is now commonly used as a business development tool and can offer effective, rapid and stimulating ways of enhancing business skills and performance.

What are the common issues for many people at work? The following are some which are probably familiar to you:

- setting objectives
- planning and organizing
- solving problems and making decisions
- managing time, finance and other resources
- dealing with, and managing, others – including negotiating, interviewing, counselling, appraising, running meetings and teambuilding
- training, facilitating, coaching and mentoring
- writing letters, memos and reports
- making presentations/public speaking
- carrying out research and development
- being innovative

- selling and marketing
- customer care
- personal professional development

All these topics are ones which are required across a range of work and business situations and NLP can provide ways of making them all simpler and more enjoyable. There are now many NLP books on specialist areas of business, particularly selling, negotiating, managing time, training, creativity and teambuilding, although the NLP techniques which are used in such books can apply equally to all business areas.

This chapter will take a few work- and business-related topics and show how the application of NLP can improve personal and group success. The topics we will be covering in some depth are:

- objective setting
- time management
- planning and organizing
- negotiating
- continuing professional development

We will return at the end of the chapter to considering how NLP can also be applied to the other business topics mentioned above.

OBJECTIVE SETTING

In your work, you will probably have found that it is easier to achieve results if you have a clear idea of what you are aiming for. There is a commonly used business acronym, SMART, which stands for five things which are useful in objective setting; the letters represent:

- specific
- measurable
- achievable
- realistic
- time-based

All these things are important in objective setting and NLP has taken this process further with what is called 'Well Formedness'. In NLP, people are encouraged to strive for what are termed Well Formed Outcomes or WFO for short (*see also* chapter 1).

There are several elements to the Well Formedness model and the most commonly described are:

- **Stating what you want in a positive manner**. The principle behind this is that objectives should be stated positively rather than negatively. So, for example, when shopping most people tend to make lists of the things they want to buy, rather than the things they wish to avoid. It is extremely hard to work towards a goal which is stated negatively (for example, 'I don't want to be anxious when making a presentation'). Once you know how you do want to be in presentations (eg confident and calm), you stand a better chance of working towards, and then achieving, it.
- **Thinking about the context surrounding what you want to achieve**. This means that it helps to define where and when and how you wish your objective to apply. For example, if you want to arrange a meeting, it helps to define which people need to be there, where it will be held, the duration of the event, who will lead and record it and the degree of formality that is required.
- **Striving to achieve the appropriate level of result**. When an objective is set, it is important to know the actual target to be aimed for and to check it is the real target and not simply a step on the way. So, if you want to improve the productivity of a work unit, the level of result might include the percentage increase needed and the quality required. You will need to check that the level set is not too high, so you have too much of the product left over, and not too low so that you have too little to distribute. Equally, it is important to check that the real objective is the productivity increase rather than, for example, to enhance your image in the eyes of senior management. If the real objective is different, there may be better ways of achieving it.

- **Working out the advantages and disadvantages**. This might seem self-explanatory, but the NLP approach here is to consider what are called 'secondary gains'. The idea of secondary gains is that people often gain hidden benefits from situations remaining unchanged. An objective could be to improve job clarity and make job descriptions more detailed and explicit. However, a hidden benefit in not doing this could be that people take on tasks which are not always defined and, if job descriptions were tightened up, it could stifle flexibility and innovation. So, when considering your objective, do work out whether there are any negative consequences of making the change and any hidden benefits in staying as you are.

- **Considering the 'ecology', or the circumstances surrounding the goal**. Ecology is a term commonly used in NLP, which concerns the need to check that decisions taken, or changes made, are appropriate. To this end, it is important to consider the feasibility of the steps to be taken, whether the objective is actually achievable, whether what is planned is in accordance with other elements of the situation, such as cultural traditions/norms and the personal beliefs and attitudes of those involved.

- **Being able to measure results**. This is another important element and relates to both measurement and standards. If you do not know how to assess the results of your effort, it becomes hard to set an effective objective. If you say, for example, that you wish to be better organized, this is a very vague objective. Once you begin to define it in terms of measures, things improve. So two measures of 'being better organized' could be keeping your desk top clear (which you can assess by whether or not you can see any papers on it), and managing your time better (which you could measure by the amount of time you spend in unnecessary activities and also by the number of people who tell you your time is well spent). The rather different element which NLP brings to measurement consists of personal measures, such as what you can see, hear and feel once you achieve results, as well as purely statistical measurements.

- **Assessing the degree of control you actually have**. This is an interesting point, and one with which NLP is much concerned. People often aspire to things which are beyond their control; for example other people behaving in a particular way. It is possible, for example, to say you would like someone to stop being aggressive towards you, but this is unlikely to be within your control. Better to say you would like to be able to handle the person's aggression so that you can respond to it in a positive manner; this is within your control and more likely, therefore, to be achieved. And, of course, by exerting control over your own responses, it is much more likely that the other person will be influenced to respond in a different way.
- **Gathering the resources required**. It is difficult to achieve an objective without adequate resources, and the most obvious resources at work include money, equipment and people. In NLP, however, there are other resources which need to be considered. These include personal skills and experience; they also include positive beliefs and attitudes, confidence, motivation and similar elements of thought and feeling.
- **Knowing yourself**. The importance of an objective being in keeping with a person's self-concept and personal values is vital. If you try to achieve something because you are told you should, because others achieve that thing or because you feel it is what you ought to be doing, there is less chance of it being successful. So self-analysis and awareness is a key to achieving results. (*See* chapter 4 for more on developing self-awareness.)

Time Management

We all have the same amount of time each day – 24 hours – yet:

- some people manage to achieve a good deal in that time and others achieve less
- some people find the time passes rapidly and others find it passes slowly

111

- some people feel overwhelmed by what they have to do in their time, while others feel they have all the time in the world for their tasks

What makes the difference?

This is where NLP offers more than conventional time management training. Time management skills are simple to learn and straightforward to apply, yet many people do not apply them. This is probably because what counts is not just knowing the techniques to use, but having the motivation to use them. NLP can help you focus on your perception of time and your attitudes and approaches to how you manage your time.

ATTITUDES TOWARDS TIME

Here is a small test. Look at your desk, if you have one. See if there are any items there which need dealing with, but which remain untouched. Now consider any messages these deferred tasks are sending you. For each postponed activity, there is probably an associated communication; do any of these sound familiar?

- You don't like dealing with me.
- You find me boring.
- You don't know where or how to start with me.
- You don't think you can handle me.
- Last time you dealt with me you messed things up.

Now it is possible that the only reason some of your tasks have not been completed is because you genuinely have not had time to do them. It is also likely that some of them will have been set aside for one of the reasons above – or something similar. In other words, it is your attitudes towards, your beliefs about, or your thoughts and feelings in connection with, the tasks which have prevented you from doing them.

With NLP you can analyse your attitudes, beliefs, thoughts and feelings in order to find out how they are affecting your behaviour and thereby your achievements (*see* the section on the Experiential Array in chapter 1 for more on this). Unless you tackle some of these issues it is unlikely that you will have the motivation and perseverance to start and complete the necessary tasks.

So find out what message each of the unfinished tasks is sending you and then ask yourself some questions about the task, such as 'Do I want to do this?', 'Do I need to do this?', 'Is this worth doing?' Once you have your answers to the questions, you can decide whether to tackle the task and, if you do decide to go ahead with it, NLP can offer you ways of getting there.

So, taking the five points above, let us see how NLP can help.

- **Not liking a task**. If you do not like *doing* a task, you could imagine *having done it*. This shifts your perspective into a future time, after it has been done, when you can picture it completed and imagine how good you will feel when it is finished. To do this, you can use visualization to picture the task successfully completed.
- **Finding it boring**. With this one, you can search for a challenge in the task, such as seeing how quickly you can complete it. An alternative would be to give yourself a reward for completing the task in a set time – you could then look forward to the reward instead of avoiding the task.
- **Not knowing where to start**. Here, you can use the 'chunking' technique described below under 'Planning and Organizing', to sort the activity into its component elements and see it in context. Once you have read the section on chunking you can return to this item, knowing more about the technique which can be applied.
- **Thinking you cannot handle it**.This is possibly to do with self-concept and the techniques we discussed in chapter 4, on self-esteem, could help here. Using positive 'internal dialogue' can really help in boosting your confidence. Alternatively, you could think of situations in the past where you *have* handled equally challenging tasks successfully and use them to boost your belief in your capabilities.

- **Being worried about doing it badly**. By thinking in this way, you are focusing on what you do not want to happen, rather than on what you would like as a positive result. As we saw when considering objectives, the first important thing is to be able to specify your targets in a positive manner. So two things come in here; the first is the focus on avoidance and the second is how your mind recalls a previous experience of things not going well. To tackle the first, you can refocus yourself on the positive things you could do to ensure success. To tackle the second, you can work on altering your mental images, sounds or feelings to positive ones instead of negative, as we have illustrated previously.

PERCEPTION OF TIME

NLP can help give you the sense of having more time available to complete what you have to do. Think about being stuck in a traffic jam, being in the dentist's chair or having to wait for a much-anticipated letter. How slowly does time seem to pass in these situations? Now think about how time passes at weekends, at times when you are reading a good book, or when you are taking part in an exciting activity. How fast does time go now? Probably your perception of the passage of time differs between the first kind of activity and the second. Everyone has their own situations where time seems to drag on interminably and situations where things seem to be over in a flash; being able to change your perception of time so that it apparently slows down can reduce any sense of pressure and make you feel more relaxed about what you have to do.

So what makes the difference between time passing quickly or slowly?

The only thing that changes is your own perception of the time as it passes (or, in many cases, your lack of perception of the time as it passes). As the time passes, your mind is doing things such as showing you pictures, producing sounds and giving you feelings; and these will be different for situations which you code as 'interesting or exciting' and those which you code as 'dull and tedious'.

In *The Dance of Life* (Anchor Books, New York, 1983), a fascinating book about the nature of time, ET Hall describes an experiment by Alton de Long into the perception of time. In the experiment, people were asked to sit in front of miniaturized environments (like a doll's house room), imagine they were a figure in that environment carrying out some activity, and then tell the experimenters when half an hour had passed. The curious thing is that their perception of time related directly to the reduction in size of their environment, so that in a $^1/_{12}$ size environment they perceived that half an hour had passed in 2.44 minutes and in a $^1/_{24}$ size environment they perceived half an hour to have passed in 1.36 minutes. Hall deduced:

> Time and space are functionally interrelated . . . The perception of time is . . . also influenced by the scale of the environment . . . Under proper conditions, subjects will increase interaction rates in an environment to stay in agreement with the scale of that environment . . . The brain speeds up in direct proportion to environmental scale.

It would appear, according to Hall, that it should be possible to accomplish certain kinds of decision-making tasks in an enormously reduced time as well as giving an individual up to 12 hours' experience in the course of an hour!

So perception of time is not a fixed element, but can vary according to both the attitudes of the person and the environment in which the person is functioning. NLP has many ways of working with perception of time and two of the best known are:

- time lines
- time distortion

The idea of **time lines** (a very old concept, as we mentioned in chapter 3) is that people are able to distinguish between events happening in the past, present and future, not only cognitively but also representationally. In chapter 3 we considered the possibility of being able to review situations from different points in time; in this chapter we will extend this approach into how you, as an individual, represent time to

115

yourself. Have a go at the following exercise to demonstrate how this can come about.

Think about a particular event which occurred some time ago – say five or ten years. Choose an event which left a lasting memory. As you think of the event, notice whether your attention is drawn in any particular direction (to one side of yourself, in front or behind you, high up or low down and so forth) or whether your focus of attention is internal. Repeat this process, thinking next of another memorable event in the more recent past (say a few days ago), then an event which is likely to occur in the next few days, and finally an event which is likely to take place some years hence. In each case, notice where your attention is drawn.

Once you have a location for each event, draw an imaginary line joining them all up. Each person will have a unique way of representing these connections and it has been noticed that there are some common ways. The most common are lines which are out in front of a person (say from left to right) and lines which run through the person (generally from front to back). NLP calls the first concept that of 'through time' and the second concept that of 'in time'.

As far as time management goes, it seems that 'through time' people, ie those who perceive time as if it is visible in front of them, tend to be well organized and aware of time as it passes (punctual and reliable). 'In time' people are immersed in time; for them past, present and future are all interconnected and they tend to be less aware of the passage of time and less concerned with its significance; they may be late for appointments and find it hard to complete tasks to schedule.

So if you wish to improve your time management, it helps to become more aware of the tasks and activities as external to yourself and, where possible, to 'see' them in front of you – noticing their component parts, how they relate to other tasks you have to undertake and so forth. By giving projects a kind of embodiment, and seeing them clearly, it is easier to make them tangible and get a sense of how long they will take to do and how to approach them.

Time distortion is a technique which is much used in hypnotherapy, and NLP therapists find it a useful way of assisting people to feel as though they have more time when under pressure and, conversely, have time speeded up when it could potentially drag, such as going to the dentist's or waiting in a traffic jam. The process consists of getting into a highly relaxed state and giving yourself (or, more usually, being given) suggestions, often via an imaginary scenario, that time is passing either faster or slower. For example, you might be asked to imagine how slowly time may seem to pass when you are waiting in a supermarket queue and then be helped to transfer that feeling of time slowing down into a work situation when you need to have the feeling that more time is available. These techniques are extremely effective (and similar to ones which are used for the control of perception of pain); if you wish to know more, NLP practitioners and psychotherapists are the people to contact (for how to do this, *see* Useful Addresses).

PLANNING AND ORGANIZING

All of us need to plan at some time in our lives. Having techniques to help with this process is a great aid to effectiveness.

An NLP technique which is very helpful in planning and organizing is called 'chunking', which was covered briefly in chapter 3. Chunking is a process whereby activities may be analysed and tackled in a systematic way. Using chunking, it is possible to see any activity in its full context. Let us take an example of a work issue and see how chunking could be applied to it.

Suppose you have to plan and organize a meeting concerned with an office relocation. Let us represent the meeting as a box, shown below:

```
┌─────────────────────┐
│    Meeting on        │
│  office re-location  │
└─────────────────────┘
```

It could be easy to see the meeting out of context, ie as a self-contained event. However, the meeting is only one event in the relocation process. Because the overall process is bigger than the meeting, we can add it, above the original box, to our diagram as follows:

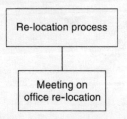

Now, let us consider the meeting in a broader context. This meeting is on relocation, but other meetings may need to take place on general business finance and on competition from other businesses; these meetings are equivalent in significance to the relocation meeting and can, therefore, be added to the diagram at the same level, as follows:

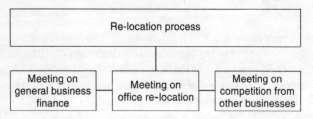

Finally, let us take the meeting itself and consider what elements it comprises. Some components of the meeting could be as follows:

- the people to be invited
- the time the meeting is to be held
- the venue for the meeting
- the documentation needed to be prepared
- any refreshments to be provided
- how minutes will be taken

All these are sub-elements of the meeting and can also be added to the diagram as sub-parts as follows:

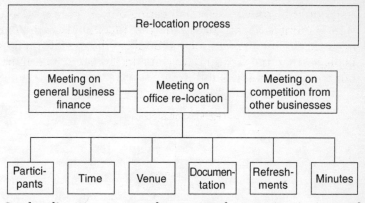

So the diagram we now have puts the meeting in its total context.

The chunking process allows you to think about the component elements of any situation and to represent them in diagrammatic form. Once you have analysed them in this way, it becomes easier to see inter-relationships and to separate out each of the activities you need to complete.

NEGOTIATING

There are many work situations where negotiation is necessary. Some people are professional negotiators, for example involved in industrial relations, estate agency or car sales. Others simply negotiate as part of their everyday work activities – negotiating lunchtime cover for themselves, negotiating more time to complete a report, negotiating their salary level. For all these situations, there are NLP techniques which can facilitate acceptable outcomes. Rackham and Carlisle (Journal of European Industrial Training, 1978) described the characteristics of effective negotiators. One of these characteristics was the ability to predict objections, changes of mind or other obstacles to successful implementation and to take action early on to forestall them. NLP has a term for dealing with such events; it is known as 'future pacing'. Future pacing involves considering future scenarios in an effort to both predict and successfully handle them. Let us take a negotiating situation and see how future pacing might help it.

Suppose you are responsible for getting together a working party to see through a project. You know what has to be done and simply have to make sure you have the right people for the task. You need five people and can select from ten available. The ten are as follows (note: some of the descriptions below are loosely based on Meredith Belbin's team roles work and some take into account the NLP meta-programme categories):

1 Very bright, fast, energetic; tends to dominate meetings and bulldoze people who do not work at the same speed

2 Very good at detail, reliable and good at spotting mistakes; tends to hold things up while checking minor points

3 Good at seeing the 'big picture'; does not like having to work on fine detail

4 Excellent at dealing with others, networking and getting information; tends to spend a lot of time chatting and exploring options

5 Always comes up with good ideas; sometimes a bit too off the wall

6 Good at keeping everyone focused on the job in hand; sometimes ignores other options which could be even more helpful

7 A good technical person who knows about the subject area in question; not so good at understanding others' interests and involvements

8 Very positive and goal-focused; sometimes does not see obstacles in the way

9 A good time manager; sometimes takes short cuts in order to keep to schedule

10 Good at finding resources, sources of information and supplies; sometimes keener on the hunt for material than on the job in hand

Now, using future pacing, you could predict outcomes for different combinations of people on your project and think through what would happen with different groupings. For example:

- What if I had the quick thinker, the person taking an overview and the contact person together with the detail person and the technical expert? How would they get on and what would I have to do to keep them all together? How would it feel to be part of that group? Would we meet our timescales or would we be held up by internal conflict?
- If I have the ideas person in the group, will it help or hinder? How would the others handle that person more outrageous suggestions produced?
- Would the addition of a networking person be an asset; would that person spend too much time on creating relationships inside and outside the group rather than getting on with the job?

What future pacing adds to this kind of assessment is the ability to imagine the future 'as if you are in it right now'. So you can imagine how it would feel to be in meetings with the particular grouping of people you have in mind, you can imagine hearing the kind of conversations which would go on and you can imagine what will or will not get done as a result.

So future pacing can help you answer questions such as: 'Is it appropriate to take this course of action', 'What would it actually be like in that situation?', 'How will people respond?' and so forth. And an NLP question to remember when considering the future is 'Is it ecological?' – in other words, do all the elements involved work harmoniously, are they ethical, and are all the components congruent (or consistent) with each other?

CONTINUING PROFESSIONAL DEVELOPMENT

Finally let us consider how you can extend your own personal development within a work context. Continuing professional development (CPD) is a term much in use at present. CPD is now a requirement which most professional bodies make of their members as they recognize the importance of keeping up with a rapidly changing business world. If you are keen to enhance your own professional knowledge and skills on a continuing basis, you may well be helped by NLP's emphasis on modelling, which we have mentioned in earlier chapters.

In a business context, modelling is about noticing which people are achieving excellent results and then adopting – in a modified form if necessary – some elements of what they do (specifically the elements which produce the difference between competence and *excellence* in performance). As we saw in chapter 1, NLP is concerned with objectives, behaviour, mental strategy, emotional state, beliefs, values and assumptions, all operating within a specific context. If you wish to develop your own abilities, you can find out how high performers in your own field achieve their results by finding out their ways of dealing with each of these elements.

Let's take an example to illustrate how you might go about this. Suppose you want to promote an idea or product of yours. Find one or more people who you know are successful at promotional activities and begin to work out how they get their results. This is the process which Bandler and Grinder embarked upon in the early days of NLP.

To find out how these people act in such a successful way, you will need to ask them questions and/or observe them in operation. Here are some of the possible questions you might ask concerning the performance elements we considered above.

Objectives
- *What* do you want to *achieve* when you promote an idea/product?

Behaviour
- What do you *do* first when promoting something new?
- *How* do you contact potential consumers?
- *When* do you contact people? What time of day? What day of the week?
- What do you *say* to them?
- Do you *telephone* them first?
- Do you *write* to them? If so, at what stage?
- When meeting potential consumers, how do you *behave*? What do you *wear*? How do you *speak*?

- What *posture* do you adopt? How do you *shake hands*?
- What kind of *promotional material* do you use? How does it *look*? What does it *say*?

Mental strategy

- What goes on *in your mind* as you consider promotional activities?
- Do you *visualize the outcome* you want?
- Do you *imagine* meetings with consumers going well?
- Do you *tell yourself* they will be interested?
- Do you *imagine hearing them* sounding interested?

Emotional state

- How do you *feel* when you consider promoting something?
- What *state* are you in just before meeting a potential consumer?
- What *state* are you in during the meeting?
- Do you deliberately create a particular *emotion* in yourself at any stage in the process? If so, *what* is it?
- How do you *feel* when you have been successful in a promotional activity?

Beliefs, values and attitudes

- What do you *believe* about the idea/product you are promoting?
- How *valuable* do you think the idea/product is?
- How *interested* do you think the consumer/s will be?
- What do you *believe* about your own ability to promote the idea/product?
- What do you *assume* about other people's responses?
- What is your *attitude* towards the consumer/s?

- Is there *anything else* you would like to tell me which is important to you about this process?

This list of questions should give you an idea of how to approach the process of modelling. What you are aiming for is as complete a picture as you can get of how the person functions in the particular context and especially the elments which distinguish excellence from competence. If you can also observe this person in action it is likely to be helpful. If you can question and observe several people in the same kind of situation it should also give you an idea of how approaches can vary and, importantly, what they have in common. In a modelling project I carried out on management consultants in 1993, to find out about those who were good at converting business prospects into actual assignments, some common features of the most successful were:

- they were very more proactive
- they were more client-centred than self-centred
- their objectives were more to do with resolving problems and educating their clients, whereas the less effective ones' objectives were more to do with getting business and not wasting time
- they treated client interactions as partnerships, shared ventures and learning experiences
- they were more persistent and found the experience a personal challenge
- they had much more positive feelings, stressed the need to generate energy, to think positively and to respond to challenges, they enjoyed dealing with their clients and said it was important to counter negative feelings and create 'the right frame of mind'. (In contrast, those who did not do so well felt exasperated by non-responding clients, felt the clients were 'useless and incompetent', felt negative and angry about them and said it was not worth the 'hassle' to deal with them)
- they were much more concerned with the big picture than with detail
- they kept better records of client contact

So it is possible to build up a good picture of what makes for success and then, if appropriate, train yourself or others to achieve similar results. NLP does not have the monopoly on role modelling but, because of its attention to the 'small chunks' of experience and perception, it has ways of describing excellence that are not often found elsewhere.

At the start of this chapter, we discussed various business-related topics and selected a small number to which NLP techniques could be applied. We have not explored all the topics mentioned, although some of them have been referred to briefly in other chapters of the book. There are many NLP techniques which can be used in all these business-related areas and, to remind you of some which can be useful, the following list is of the remaining topics, together with some suggestions of NLP techniques you might use in each area:

- **Problem solving and decision making**. These topics can be approached using chunking, TOTE diagrams, the Disney Strategy and future pacing.
- **Dealing with and managing other people**. Useful techniques in this area include observation skills, rapport creation and maintenance, language skills, shifts of perspective and recognition of/respect for others' beliefs and values.
- **Training, presenting, facilitating, coaching and mentoring**. Techniques you could consider include Accelerated Learning (identification of and responding to variation in learning styles), anchoring of positive states, use of indirect language and role modelling.
- **Business writing**. This can be helped by matching readers' sensory preferences (using appropriate sensory-specific language, paper texture, graphics, etc), matching their motivational patterns by using appropriate meta-programmes and influencing through the use of indirect language and embedded instructions.
- **Research, development and innovation**. Helpful techniques could include the use of the Disney Strategy and time lines to generate ideas and evaluate options.
- **Sales and marketing**. Results could be improved by considering customers' values and criteria in relation to products and services being promoted. Sales performance could be enhanced by generating positive thoughts and feelings before embarking on a sales activity.
- **Customer care**. Here it is important to understand the customer's perspective, use language which makes the

customer feel valued and listened to and maintain positive states in order to remain resourceful when dealing with criticism, hostility or disappointment.

Although there are many techniques you can use, if you are flexible and selective, you will be able to select approaches which work well for you, whatever your own area of activity, and should improve your results as a consequence.

So this final chapter has covered some techniques which can improve work performance. All the techniques are cross-contextual and likely to produce effects in more than one area of your life. So increasing your confidence can enhance your relationships, improving your relationships can make your working life easier and improving your business skills can give you more of a sense of achievement and self-worth. By using the techniques illustrated in these three applications chapters, you will be able to create a positive approach and achieve results in all areas of your life. As we said at the start, you have probably been 'doing NLP' already; the ideas in this book can help you continue to do it successfully and with enthusiasm.

SECTION THREE

This section of the book is about practical ways in which you can pursue your interest in NLP if you choose to do so. You will find the following topics covered:

- how to find out more about NLP
- NLP organizations
- how to find out about NLP training
- how to find an NLP practitioner or therapist who can help with your personal needs
- how to contact others interested in or involved with NLP
- NLP training levels/terms
- resources for study – books, video and audiotapes, magazines
- commonly used NLP terms and phrases
- references to sources used in this book

If you are new to NLP, you may find it easier to have someone help you learn and develop. Although many of the NLP processes are easy to explain in a book, others are more complex and it is helpful to have some guidance or support when working with them. It is also useful to have another person who can bring a different perspective to things; for example letting you know what they observe about you as you practise the different activities. If you do not have a friend or colleague who can help you, there are various established groups where you can find people with a similar interest in the topic.

FURTHER
INFORMATION GUIDE

There are various levels of training in NLP, which are recognized internationally. The training programmes you are most likely to come across are the following:

- **Introductory courses**. These can take anything from half a day to a week. Sometimes a certificate is given which may count towards the next level of training.
- **Practitioner training**. This is a course providing training in the basic skills, knowledge and attitudes of NLP. It may be anything from seven to 20+ days' duration, usually in a modular format, sometimes including distance learning elements. The only Practitioner courses presently recognized by the Association for Neuro-Linguistic Programming (ANLP) are those of 20 days' duration, as it is felt that, for effective skills acquisition, very short periods of study are inadequate.
- **Master Practitioner training**. This is an advanced course, building on the skills learned at Practitioner level. It is also normally modular in format and of varying lengths and

formats. As with Practitioner training, currently, the ANLP only recognizes courses of 20 days' duration.

- **Trainer training**. This is at a more advanced level, aimed at those needing skills in training others.

If you are interested in training personally, an introductory course is recommended first, to see how you get on with the subject; you can then proceed to Practitioner training if you find it to your liking.

It is helpful to contact a range of organizations before deciding where to train and, where possible, to attend introductory evenings or workshops to get a feel for how they work. Often introductory evenings are offered free of charge, or at very low cost, to give potential participants an understanding and feel for how the organization functions.

CONTACT WITH OTHERS INVOLVED IN NLP

If you are interested in NLP, but are not yet certain whether you would like to undertake formal training, it is worth joining, or starting, a practice group. Such groups can provide networking and practice opportunities to those attending. At these groups you can meet others with similar interests, hear speakers on different aspects of NLP and experience some of the NLP processes in person. *See* Useful Addresses for more details.

GLOSSARY OF NLP TERMS

This is a straightforward explanation of some commonly used NLP terms. Some of these words may be familiar to you from everyday usage, but NLP has occasionally given them different meanings, so please take this into account in reading the glossary.

Accessing cues. Movements or gestures which give an indication of the mental processes a person is using. Observation of external behaviour can give an idea of whether a person is using a particular sense (sight, hearing, touch, taste or smell) and the indicators of these include eye movements (eye accessing cues – eg looking up when visualising an image or looking down when experiencing a strong emotion), hand gestures and posture. Research (notably by Eric Robbie; UK) has shown that this process can be extended into understanding the really fine detail (Sub-modalities – *see below*) of how a person is thinking. For example whether they are making large or small pictures in their mind, seeing images in colour or black and white and so forth.

Acuity. Good observation skills. Examples: noticing that someone's breathing has become faster; becoming aware of changes in voice tone as a person speaks.

Analogue. Using a movement, gesture or vocal change to reinforce something that is said. Examples: pointing to an object while mentioning it; saying 'I would like you to go to the shops *now*', and making the word 'now' stand out by emphasizing it through a different voice tone.

Anchor. The association of a signal with a response. Examples: recalling a memory on hearing a tune; feeling confident when wearing a business suit.

Association/dissociation. Being immersed in your feelings (association); being detached from yourself, as if you were an observer (dissociation). Examples: listening to music and becoming absorbed in the experience (association); becoming aware of your tone of voice as you are speaking to someone (dissociation).

Auditory. Real or imagined use of the sense of hearing. Examples: speaking on the telephone; imagining your own voice in your head.

Calibration. Making sense of another person's behaviour through observation of the detail of what she is doing, especially non-verbal elements. This is then used as a reference base for further observations. Examples: hearing a person's voice speed up on the phone could be an indication that they wish to end the conversation, if you have already 'calibrated' the speed of their voice in comparable situations; noticing a person's facial expression can indicate whether they are interested in a subject, regardless of whether they say anything about it.

Chunking (up or down). Taking either a broad view or a more detailed perspective in order to achieve a result. Examples: if two colleagues are in dispute about where to site a piece of office equipment, *chunking up* by asking them to consider how other people might also be affected by the decision (ie broadening the discussion); if a friend has become tired of how a room is decorated and wants to make a change, but does not know where to start, *chunking down* by asking him what colour is preferred, how much money there is to spend, whether paper or paint is desired, etc (ie getting him to focus on the detail rather than the room as a whole).

Congruence/incongruence. The presence (congruence) or absence (incongruence) of consistency between what a person says and/or does. Examples: someone saying she dislikes a particular food and, at the same time screwing up her face (congruence); someone telling you she has enjoyed a particular film at the same time as shaking her head (incongruence).

Criteria. Things which are important to people; what they value. Examples: 'When I choose a television I want it to have a good design (criterion) and be affordable (criterion)'; 'What is important to me in a job is the responsibility (criterion) I have and the distance (criterion) from my home'.

Dissociation. *See* Association.

Ecology. Taking into account the circumstances or context surrounding an action, so that its appropriateness and impact may be assessed. Examples: taking into account the impact on a child's learning and circle of friends before deciding whether a house move should take place; considering whether the higher salary produced by a job change justifies the additional stress the job might generate.

Future pacing. Imagining how something will be in the future; trying it out in your mind. Examples: visualizing a room painted yellow and thinking how your existing furniture will look in it; rehearsing a speech at a business event, as if the audience were already there and imagining how it will feel at the time.

Gustatory. The real or imagined use of the sense of taste. Examples: eating a biscuit; imagining the taste of a biscuit.

Incongruence. *See* Congruence.

Kinaesthetic. The real or imagined use of the sense of touch and emotion. Examples: stroking a piece of velvet and feeling the softness of the fabric; remembering the feeling of excitement of winning a race.

Lead system. The sense (sight, hearing, touch, taste or smell) which a person tends to favour. Can be observed through their unconscious eye movements, and also assessed through their language (Predicates – *see below*), sometimes referred to as 'primary system' rather than 'lead system'. Examples: needing to see the dessert trolley in a restaurant in order to decide what to choose could indicate a visual preference; needing to 'have a go' when assembling equipment, rather than reading the instructions, could indicate a kinaesthetic preference.

Matching. Copying a small part of a person's behaviour. Matching helps gain rapport, as people tend to feel comfortable with someone who comes across as similar to themselves. Examples: wearing formal clothes for an occasion when other people will be dressed similarly; smiling when a person smiles at you. Matching is sometimes referred to as 'mirroring', although this literally means copying exactly, a process which is not generally necessary.

Meta. Denoting something which is beyond or above other things. In NLP the main use of this term is in relation to personal interactions and use of language. Examples: meta position – a perspective which is beyond an interaction, for example talking to someone while imagining being 'a fly on the wall'; meta state – an emotional state beyond another emotional state, for example feeling *angry* about being *afraid* of heights, or feeling *guilty* about being *lethargic*.

Meta-Model/Milton Model. The two best known NLP language models. The Meta Model is about using language in a precise and explicit manner and the Milton Model is about using language in an indirect manner, which can influence or guide experience. Examples: to boil an egg you need to put the egg in a saucepan, completely cover the egg with cold water, bring it to the boil, turn the heat down until it simmers and wait three minutes until the egg is cooked through but still soft with a runny yolk (Meta-Model); it is easy to boil an egg; just cook it until it is the way you like it (Milton Model).

Meta-programme. Patterns of acting or reacting which an individual tends to prefer in given situations. Examples: relying on your own opinions ('internal' Meta-programme) rather than wanting feedback from others ('external' Meta-programme); aiming for a goal ('towards' meta-programme) rather than avoiding an obstacle ('away from' meta-programme). Meta-programmes may change across time and context, for any particular person.

Milton Model. *See* Meta-Model.

Mirroring. *See* Matching.

Modelling. Analysing a person's way of being and doing so that it can be understood and, if appropriate, copied by someone else. Examples: observing someone chair a meeting effectively, working out what precisely they do to make it go well and then doing something similar yourself; finding out about a person's non-observable characteristics in a particular situation (eg their thoughts, feelings, attitudes and beliefs) to understand what motivates them and how they react to the circumstances.

Olfactory. The real or imagined use of the sense of smell. Examples: smelling a rose; remembering the smell of a bad egg.

Outcome. An objective you wish to attain or the actual results you are achieving. Examples: *wanting* to ride a bicycle; missing a train and, as a result, *having more time* to sit on the platform and read a book.

Pacing. Continuing to match (*see* matching) another person or people as they change their behaviour. Examples: smiling as a friend tells you of a happy event and, having a serious face, tells you of something which is a problem; responding by speeding up the way you speak when an angry customer telephones and then slowing your voice as the person calms down a little.

Perceptual positions. The different perspectives we can adopt when considering a situation. An infinite number of perceptual positions could exist, but three are generally described. Examples: being so engrossed in an activity that you do not hear someone calling to you (being in *first position*, or totally 'in your own experience'); feeling a friend's anxiety on going to a job interview (being in *second position* or imagining what the other person's experience is like); thinking how you and the other members of your family seem as a group to visitors arriving for a meal (being in *third position* – sometimes called *Meta-position*, as it is beyond the interaction itself or imagining how you and others seem to an outside observer).

Predicates. Words which relate to the use of the different senses (sight, sound, touch, taste, smell). Examples: clear, bright (predicates of *sight*); loud, squeaky (predicates of *sound*); heavy, smooth (predicates of *touch*); sweet, bitter (predicates of *taste*); acrid, musty (predicates of *smell*). *See also* representational systems.

Presuppositions. Assumptions which may or may not be valid, but are used to inform behaviour. Examples: saying 'When are you going to see the film?' presupposes the person will see it at some stage; cooking a meal for visitors presupposes they will be prepared to eat it.

Rapport. A state which exists when people are getting on well with each other. Often observable by the fact that some aspects of the people's behaviour is similar (*see* Matching). Examples: two people walking down the street side by side will often take steps at the same time; it is often easier to share silence with someone when you are in rapport with them than when you are not.

Reframing. Taking a different perspective on a situation. Examples: seeing a delay on your train as an opportunity to catch up on reading, rather than become annoyed; taking a critical comment as an opportunity to improve, rather than being upset.

Representational systems. The five senses (sight, sound, touch, taste, smell). NLP gives these senses particular names: *visual* (sight); *auditory* (sound – and *auditory digital* is sometimes used as a term for a person who has imaginary conversations in her head); *kinaesthetic* (touch – and also emotional feeling); *gustatory* (taste); *olfactory* (smell). In NLP, the term 'representational systems' is often used to denote the *imaginary* use of the senses; for example visualizing or having a conversation in your head. Examples: visualizing yourself driving a new car; imagining the sound of a dog barking.

State. The experiencing of a particular emotion. Examples: being confident (a resourceful state); feeling depressed (an unresourceful state).

Sub-modalities. The elements of each sense. For example, when using our sense of sight we can observe colours as light or dark, and we can make mental pictures which are colourful or dull; when using our sense of hearing we can hear sounds which are loud or soft, or can imagine sounds which are sharp or muffled.

Synaesthesia. The simultaneous experience of more than one sensory process ('synthesizing of the senses'). This can involve the representation of one sensory experience through a different sensory channel or a representation in one sensory system eliciting an associated response in another system. Examples: 'seeing' different colours as you hear different musical notes; having a particular taste in your mouth as you feel the shape of a certain object.

Visual. The real or imagined use of the sense of sight. Examples: looking at pictures in an exhibition; picturing, in your mind, what a tree will look like once its leaves have fallen off.

BIBLIOGRAPHY AND OTHER RESOURCES

Introductory

Introducing Neuro-Linguistic Programming – A good basic text, systematic and comprehensive (British). O'Connor and Seymour. HarperCollins. 1990.

NLP The New Technology of Achievement – Practical, serious, exploration of aspects of NLP. Andreas and Faulkner. Nicholas Brealey. 1996.

The Magic of NLP Demystified – An easy to read introduction to the subject. Lewis and Pucelik. Metamorphous Press. 1990.

Unlimited Power – A popular exposition of many NLP concepts and techniques. Robbins. Simon and Schuster. 1988.

Neuro-Linguistic Programming Volume 1: The Study of the Structure of Subjective Experience – An early text on NLP concepts. Dilts, Grinder, Bandler, DeLozier. Meta Publications. 1978.

Frogs into Princes – The book that started it all; early NLP workshop transcripts. Bandler and Grinder. Real People Press. 1979.

Using your Brain for a Change – An introduction to Sub-Modalities. Entertaining introduction to the topic. Bandler. Real People Press. 1985.

NLP: The Wild Days – A short personal account of NLP's origins. McClendon. Meta Publications. 1989.

General

Leaves Before the Wind – Collected writings on NLP applications and developments. Bretto et al. Grinder, DeLozier and Associates. 1991.

NLP Personal Profile – Tests and questionnaires to help you identify your own styles. Engel and Arthur. Life Star. 1995.

In and Out the Garbage Pail – Fritz Perls' autobiography; lively, amusing and anecdotal. Perls. The Gestalt Journal Press. 1992 (1969 original publication).

New Code NLP

Turtles all the Way Down – Workshop transcripts introducing New Code approaches. DeLozier and Grinder. Grinder, DeLozier and Associates. 1987.

Training

Training with NLP – A practical guide for those in training and development (British). O'Connor and Seymour. HarperCollins. 1994.

The Excellent Trainer – Information and activities for using NLP in training (British). Kamp. Gower. 1996.

40 Activities for Training with NLP – Looseleaf activities for trainers (British). Johnson. Gower. 1996.

The Creative Trainer – Accelerated Learning techniques in training (British). Lawlor and Handley. McGraw Hill. 1996.

Sales

Sales: The Mind's Side – A simple, practical guide to selling. Robertson. Metamorphous Press. 1990.

Language

Words that Change Minds – Influencing through the use of Metaprogrammes. Excellent guidance for those with or without experience in NLP. Charvet. Kendall Hunt Publishing Co. Undated.

The Structure of Magic (Volume 1) – The Meta Model explained. For the serious student; in-depth exploration of linguistic processes. Bandler and Grinder. Science and Behaviour Books. 1975.

Therapeutic Metaphors – An introduction to constructing and using metaphors. Gordon, David. Meta Publications. 1978.

Precision – NLP communications processes in business. McMaster and Grinder. Precision Models. 1980.

Business

Influencing with Integrity – NLP in work situations; meetings, negotiating, etc. Laborde. Syntony Publications. 1983.

NLP at Work – using NLP in a business context (British)*. Knight. Nicholas Brealey Publishing. 1995.

Therapy

Solutions – Practical NLP techniques applied to relationship issues. Cameron and Bandler. Future Pace Inc. 1985.

Uncommon Therapy – Case studies of Milton Erickson. Haley. Norton. 1986.

Peoplemaking – How to make relationships work. Satir. Science and Behaviour Books. 1972.

Phoenix – Therapeutic patterns of Milton Erickson. Gordon and Mayers-Anderson. Meta Publications. 1981.

Modelling

Tools for Dreamers – Creativity and problem solving. Dilts *et al.* Meta Publications. 1991.

Strategies of Genius – Modelling excellence. Dilts. Meta Publications. 1994 onwards.

The Emprint Method – Modelling techniques. Cameron and Bandler *et al.* Real People Press. 1985.

Know How – Personal development workbook. Cameron and Bandler. Future Pace. 1985.

Time

Time Line Therapy and the Basis of Personality – Bringing about change through exploration of time. James and Woodsmall. Meta Publications. 1988.

Time Lining – Latest developments in work with time. Bodenhamer and Hall. Anglo-American Book Co. 1997.

Precursers to NLP

Science and Sanity. Korzybski. Institute of General Semantics. 1933.

Steps to an Ecology of Mind. Bateson. Ballantine Books. 1972.

Plans and the Structure of Behaviour. Miller, Galanter and Pribram.

Language and the Mind. Chomsky. Harcourt Brace College. 1972.
Psychosynthesis. Assagioli. Aquarian Press. 1993.
Psycho-Cybernetics Maltz. Prentice-Hall Inc. 1960.

Associated topics

Super Teaching NLP and Accelerated Learning Techniques – An excellent guide for teachers and trainers. Jensen. Turning Point for Teachers. 1995.

Creative Imagery – Visualization techniques. Fezler. Simon and Schuster. 1989.

OTHER RESOURCES

Audiotapes

NLP: The New Technology of Achievement – NLP skills and approaches. NLP Comprehensive and Nightingale Conant. Two-tape set.

Business Applications of NLP. Ewing. Two-tape set.

Success in Mind – NLP based personal effectiveness tapes. Titles include: 'Super Self', 'Handling Social Situations', 'Super Slimming' (British) Harris. Management Magic. 1995.

Videotapes

There are videotapes available of several of the well known figures in and around NLP, including Richard Bandler, Milton Erickson and Virginia Satir.

Magazines and journals

There is a small, but growing, number of NLP based publications throughout the world and ANLP puts details of them on its web site (see opposite). Current publications include:

- *Anchorpoint*, 346 South 500 East, Suite 200, Salt Lake City, Utah 84102, USA
- *Multimind*, Junfermannsche Verlagsbuchhandlung GmbH & Co KG, Postfach 18 40, D–33048, Paderborn, Germany
- *The NLP Connection*, PO Box 12009–168, Scottsdale, Arizona 85267, USA
- *NLP World*, Les 3 Chasseurs, 1413 Orzens, Switzerland
- *Rapport*, PO Box 78, Stourbridge, West Midlands, DY8 2YP, UK. Tel: 01384 443935 Fax: 01384 823448

Useful Addresses

The Australian Institute of NLP
c/o Askawn Quality Solutions Pty Ltd
PO Box 31
Kippa-Ring
QLD 4021
Tel: 07 3204-0824. Fax 07 3204-0825

Austria

European Association for Neruolinguistic Psychotherapy
  (EA-NLPt)
A-1094 Vienna
Widerhofergasse-4
Tel: +43 1 31767 80

Canada

Canadian Association of NLP
1715 Pilgrim's Way
Oakville
Ontario L6M 2G5
Tel: 905 469 3373 Fax: 905 469 3374
E-mail: rmilland@compuserve.com

CZECH REPUBLIC

Czech Institute for NLP
Karlovo Namesti 17
120-00 Praha 2
Czech Republic
Tel: 0042 02 2198 6280

DENMARK

The Danish NLP Institute
GL Koge Landevej 135
2500 Valby
Denmark
Tel: 0045 7010 1170

FINLAND

Juholankatu
11c, 04400
Jaruenpaa
Finland
Tel: 0358 0 2919 834

GERMANY

The German Association for NLP
Weststrasse 76
D-33615 Bielefeld
Germany
Tel: 0049 521 123 269

UNITED KINGDOM

The Association for Neuro-Linguistic Programming
PO Box 78
Stourbridge
West Midlands DY8 2YP
Tel: 01384 443935. Fax 01384 823448.
Web site: http://anlp.org

ANLP offers a range of services including:

- producing a quarterly magazine *Rapport* (free to members and available on subscription)
- running annual conferences and other events
- producing information booklets
- producing a directory of members
- having a web site for the exchange of information on NLP

Please contact ANLP if you would like to:

- know more about NLP and what is happening in the NLP community
- find out about training
- contact an NLP practitioner
- contact an NLP therapist
- find out about membership of ANLP
- find out about local practice groups
- find out how to set up a practice group

INLPTA (International Neuro-Linguistic Programming Trainers' Association)
A world wide network of trainers which sets standards and codes of ethics and has branches in a number of countries

1201 Delta Glen Court
Vienna
VA 22182
USA
Tel: 001703 757 7945 Fax: 001 703 757 7946
E-mail: wyattwoodsmall@compuserve.com

Management Magic (Carol Harris)
PO Box 47
Welshpool
Powys SY21 7NX
Wales
Tel: 01938 553430. Fax 01938 555355.
E-mail: mngt.magic@dial.pipex.com

Management Magic specialises in the development of people and organisations, runs NLP-based courses in personal and business skills, carries out personal coaching and produces audiotapes.

USA

IANLP
PO Box 12009-168
Scottsdale
AZ 85267
Tel: 001 602 835 2372
Fax: 001 602 488 3614

WEB SITES FOR NLP

The Association for Neuro-Linguistic Programming:
http://anlp.org
Modelling database (David Gordon and Graham Dawes):
www.experiential-dynamics.org
Modelling projects (Joseph O'Connor):
http://www.lambent.com
NLP research database: http://www.nlp.de/research/
Web discussion group: alt.psychology.nlp

NLP BOOK/TAPES SUPPLIERS

The Anglo-American Book Company Ltd: Crown Buildings, Bancyfelin, Carmarthen, SA33 5ND, Wales, UK. Tel: 01267 211880. Fax (UK) 01267 211882. E-mail books@american.co.uk

NLP Comprehensive: 5695 Yukon, Arunda, CO, USA, 800002. Tel: 001 303 940 8888

Credit
Some of the information on the history of NLP in the UK in chapter two was taken from various issues of *Rapport* magazine

INDEX